7 Keys *to a* Healthy *Blended* Family

Jim Smoke

HARVEST HOUSE PUBLISHERS

EUGENE, OREGON

Cover by Koechel Peterson & Associates, Inc., Minneapolis, Minnesota

Published in association with the literary agency of Alive Communications, Inc., 7680 Goddard Street, Suite 200, Colorado Springs, CO 80920

Cover photo of teenage boy © Vicky Kasala/Getty Images/Photodisc Green

Poem by Jennifer Dillion on pages 207-08 is used by permission.

Every effort has been made to give proper credit for all stories, poems, and quotations. If for any reason proper credit has not been given, please notify the author or publisher and proper notation will be given on future printing.

SEVEN KEYS TO A HEALTHY BLENDED FAMILY
Copyright © 2004 by Jim Smoke
Published by Harvest House Publishers
Eugene, Oregon 97402
www.harvesthousepublishers.com

Library of Congress Cataloging-in-Publication Data
Smoke, Jim.
    Seven keys to a healthy blended family / Jim Smoke.
        p. cm.
    Includes bibliographical references.
    ISBN 0-7369-1164-2 (pbk.)
    1. Family—Religious life. I. Title.
    BV4526.3.S65 2004
    248.8'45—dc22   2003022879

Printed in the United States of America

04 05 06 07 08 09 10 / CP-CF / 10 9 8 7 6 5 4 3 2 1

'05

To the Van Amburg family
God bless you!

Dana Lewis

To the millions of men, women, and children
living in and working hard at creating
healthy blended families

Acknowledgments

Thanks to my wife, Carol, for typing, critiquing, suggesting changes, and making this book get to the publisher in a professional manner.

Thanks to my literary agent, Greg Johnson, for his gentle nudging me along in all the books I have written under his watchful eye, this one included.

Thanks to Barbara Gordon for her masterful editing and wise input.

Thanks to the entire Harvest House Publishers family for many years of making my writing dreams turn into productive books that change people's lives.

A special thanks for all my friends living in blended families today and proving 24/7 that with God's help and hard work, blending works!

And thank you, Bob Hawkins Sr., for that luncheon way back in the early '70s when you suggested I write a book to help men and women who were going through divorce. Little did we know how God would use that book!

Contents

To the Reader

There are many ways to read a book. Most people read the words from beginning to end, decide if it was helpful or not, and move on to their next book. You will gain the most help from this book by *reading* and *responding* to it. The questions at the end of each chapter are designed specifically to help you do that.

If you can get a small group of blended family couples together, you will find it helpful to take a chapter a week and discuss the contents and questions with your group. But still write your personal plans, goals, and responses in the Journal pages.

If reading this book on your own, read one chapter at a time, respond to the questions, and write the significant things you intend to do as action steps in the Journal pages at the back of the book.

You can agree with everything in this book and yet do nothing concrete about it. The workable guidelines in this book will only make a difference in the life of your blended family if you take them off the pages and put them into practice in your life.

May God guide and direct you as you read and interact with the following pages.

Introduction

H E WASN'T WEARING A TUX, and she wasn't wearing a white bridal gown. They both looked very casual, very nervous, and very worried that they would forget the carefully crafted wedding vows they had written over the past weeks. The wedding party standing before me was made up of the bride and groom, his two boys, and her two girls. They were surrounded by a loose-knit cluster of family and friends. On this day, Mark and Linda would become husband and wife and plunge headlong into their biggest challenge ever...building and growing a blended family.

I knew as the marriage ceremony was about to begin that this day would be a day of celebration for both them and for me. I had met Mark and Linda three years earlier in a divorce recovery workshop I was offering. They had come to find the help they needed to survive their divorces. They didn't know each other at that time and were joining 80 other participants, who were broken and hurting human beings wondering if they could survive the pain, anger, betrayal, resentment, and sadness they felt. I was there with Mark and Linda in their pain and loss. I saw the slow healing catch hold in their individual lives and watched them become involved as team leaders in helping heal the hurts in other people's lives. I cheered for them as they slowly formed a close friendship. That friendship turned into love, and now they stood on the threshold of creating a new family—a blended family with all their hopes and dreams intact. And I knew this marriage could defy the odds and not only survive but thrive. Why was I so certain? Because Mark and Linda were committed to each other and to their new family...and because they would put into practice the principles in this book—principles designed to strengthen blended family unity.

The Blended Family Experience

I wholeheartedly believe that blended families can work. In my more than 28 years of ministry in the divorce/recovery field, I have talked to thousands of people who have survived the treacherous sea of divorce and successfully navigated the sometimes rocky currents of life as single parents. I've also counseled people who have lost their mates through death. Although the struggles they've gone through are different in a lot of ways, they've felt the ache of loss, too. And they've had to work through the loneliness of being alone to find the joy of single life. Happily, many of these people have now found new life partners. And as they married, they entered into the sometimes calm, sometimes choppy waters of blended families.

Every blended family situation is unique, but there are issues and attitudes that are usually found when two families merge together. I know this from my many years of ministry to hurting families and because I grew up in a blended family. My father was killed in an auto accident when I was about a year old, and my mother remarried a few years later. Soon my sister was born into this new family structure, and overnight...*kapow*...we were a newly created blended family. No one told me how different that would be.

I could never quite figure out why my father's parents seemed to always favor my sister...his blood. They seemed uncomfortable in my presence. Gifts from them to me were vastly outnumbered by the ones they gave my sister. My father's desire to spend time with me alone and make me feel special was outdistanced by his busyness with his business. His discipline when directed at me was far more severe than at my sister. I always felt that I was someone else's son and not really his. Like many children living today in stepparent situations, my mother worked hard to keep me balanced and let me know that she loved me.

When I was growing up, there were no statistical or sociological studies and no self-help books to help educate and equip me to live in this very different family system. Many years later, when I began listening to blended family stories of struggles, conflicts, and unfairness, my mind would click into gear and say, "Remember? This happened to you once." I understand some of the struggles and joys the adults and children go through when becoming a new family unit.

The failure rate of second marriages according to the U.S. Census Bureau is somewhere between 55 to 70 percent. But because I believe strongly in second marriages/ blended family adventures, I will in the following pages talk about things that work and how to implement them in building a healthy blended family. I have a large community of friends across the country who are living this story a day at a time and doing it well. I hope I can add you to my list.

No one book, or all the books combined, addressing the many complexities of a blended family will have an instant answer for your particular struggle. The seven keys to a healthy blended family I present in this book are time-tested by many blended families and are vital to survival and growth for a blended family today. Read, think, and discuss these chapters with other blended families. The seven keys—change, forgiveness, communication, compromise, acceptance, commitment, and being spiritually centered—will give you a solid foundation for constructing and maintaining a healthy blended family.

When you face particular problems, it's important to not pretend they don't exist. When the going gets tough, don't look for an exit sign and an escape route from your blended family marriage. Apply the principles in this book, pray hard, and stay the course. There are millions who share your story, and they continue to find the answers that will enable them to raise healthy and dynamic blended families.

I pray this book will be a plumb line to any and all who are thinking about creating a new blended family and those who are already living in the creation of one.

—Jim Smoke
Palm Desert, California, 2003

ONE

The Challenge of a Blended Family

Healthy things grow. Growing things change. Changing things challenge us. Challenge causes us to trust God. Trust leads to obedience. Obedience makes us healthy. And healthy things grow.

JAMES RYLE

IT WAS A CHAOTIC MORNING as Fred and Sally tried to get their five children ready for the school bus, which was due in ten minutes. Seven voices were at high decibel level as various schedules were checked, lunches were distributed, and an assortment of family animals added their erratic movements and sounds to the household din. Two children were loudly arguing over clothing choices and rightful owners. Two other children were almost in tears over misplaced homework assignments. Spilled cereal littered the kitchen as accusing voices tried to place blame. The morning noise was close to rendering ear damage when the oldest teenage boy screamed, "I hate living in this family! I want to go back to when it was just my sister, my mom, and me."

Sound familiar? The numbers in your kitchen may be smaller or greater than at Fred and Sally's, but the song is an old one, and the sound of it usually brings on a cold front of silence and the gnawing feeling in a parent that blending these two tribes may not have been such a great idea after all.

At issue in Fred and Sally's family—and thousands like them—is a simple word: change. The decision to shift gears from being a single-parent household to a blended-family household is usually made by a man and a woman. It starts when two people fall in love and sincerely believe that everything else will fall into place if they get married. In many cases, within days, weeks, or months, a couple realizes that their falling in love doesn't keep a blended family from falling apart. What tears at the fiber of a blended family so often, is not the love that a father and mother have for each other but their ability to understand and teach everyone involved in the blending process that change is a process and not an event.

In many "about to be" blended families, and even some "we are" blended families, little time has been spent honestly discussing the impending changes, how adjustments will be made, and how every family member will be impacted by them. The euphoria and excitement of creating a new family far overshadows the real struggle of the pain involved in the changes.

The seldom asked question of the children involved in blending two families is, How do you see and feel this new change coming into your life impacting and affecting you as a person? Too many adults announce their upcoming union to their children and toss the line "Are you okay with this?" at them and don't really listen to their answers. The change question merits a lot of listening and probing on the part of the parents.

I am not suggesting that children should vote on the union that will create a blended family. I am asking you, as a parent, to tune into *all* that is going on inside of your kids as they face their changes and think through what they mean to them.

The Cost of Charting a New Course

Seldom is changing a course easy. There is a cost involved. Too often we rip the price tag off, throw it away, and charge ahead. When changes hit and there is no processing or planning, chaos raises its ugly head and those involved in the changes may find themselves in a war zone. I believe the cost of any kind of course correction involves facing and answering six simple questions.

1. Are you willing to let go of the familiar in exchange for the unknown and uncertain?

We all develop carefully crafted comfort zones in which we live our daily lives. Even uncomfortable things, if lived with for a long time, can become part of our comfort zones. Habits become another comfort zone. We live in relationships with people who do things like we do. When new players with new habits invade our world, our comfort zones risk destruction. A zillion other things contribute to our comfort zones. When zones are at risk in the up-close-and-personal world of the blended family, you won't have to wait until the Fourth of July for the fireworks.

When blended families are created, things change. And there is no guaranteed way for everyone to come out on the "fair for me" side of the ledger. The win–win concept of the corporate world is a wonderful maxim, but I don't believe it's a practical reality in blended family living.

My wife and I are currently in the housing downsize challenge of life. The big house we just sold held everything and more than we possessed. The smaller one we just bought means big adjustments have to be made. Our comfort zone has been invaded, and it's time to shift gears. Fortunately, many of our decisions involve inanimate objects rather than human beings, which makes change easier. Building a blended family tends to involve both.

Riding the rapids of change in a blended family is tricky business. It demands wisdom that only God can give. Remember, in a blended family, everything goes into the blender, and what comes out isn't always what we expect.

2. Are you willing to give up any security you thought you had?

Our nation collectively has become security conscious since September 11, 2001. A visit to your local airport will quickly verify that. To most of us, the changes are both a great inconvenience and a great comfort. We want to feel secure, but we would like to do it without any personal inconvenience and disruption to our well-formed life patterns.

Security in our culture is no longer a given. Locked houses, locked cars, alarm systems, credit-card protection, and secured online computer business transactions are in place to help us feel more secure. Identity theft has invaded our once very private worlds and caused gigantic problems. And people are increasingly moving into gated communities so they will feel safe in their homes.

Feeling secure and knowing that we really are is high on most of our agendas these days. What happens when we have to give up some of the security in our lives? At best, it makes us feel tentative, uncertain, and fearful. Loss of jobs, careers, and sources of income can set off all our security alarms.

In the list of important human needs, the need for security usually comes right after the need to feel loved. Knowing you are loved brings a degree of security into your life. Knowing you are loved by all involved in a blended family can be a huge bridge-builder over the many issues and struggles of blended family living. Being loved says, "I belong." Belonging gives us a strong sense of security as blended family members.

Right about now, you are probably agreeing with me and asking yourself if all your blended family members feel loved, have a sense of belonging, and are secure in that structure. Your conclusion might be that security is about getting, not giving up.

People entering into a blended family structure give up some things that have made them feel secure as human beings. It may be a lifestyle and relationships that gave them a sense of security, which is now about to change dramatically. It may mean moving from one economic level to another. It may mean giving up one's space and personal attention from a single parent. It may mean moving to a different geographical location. Any and all things that once gave family members personal security may be on the auction block in the birth of a blended family.

Building a new security system in your life, whether as an adult or a child, takes time and a strong willingness to let go of the old and comfortable. Martyred missionary Jim Elliot summed up his feelings many years ago when he said, "He is no fool who gives what he cannot keep to gain what he cannot lose."

Lives change and structures change with them in the world of the blended family. There are no guarantees and "winners only" in this new family system. Seldom can people take everything from an old life to a new life. But loss of a sense of security from one situation can be rebuilt in another by focusing on what we are letting go of and what we need to add to our new life. There is always an "in-between time" when all we had seems lost forever, and nothing can ever make us feel secure again. The primary family is gone, and the blended family can be more of a question mark than an exclamation point. As one teenager recently said to me, "It's just not the same anymore." He was trying to find his way in a blended family that brought three other "add on" teens into his world.

Are there some magic secrets to easily giving up one kind of security and quickly finding some replacements? No! But the pathway leading from one to another has to be marked with two words: *love* and *time*. Rules, regulations, mandates, and directives never make anyone in a blended family feel secure after they have lost their personal security. Love, time, and an understanding heart will win out every time. Blended family parents need to give these to each other as well as to their children.

3. Are you willing to risk the unknown?

Those who collect and categorize human opinions tell us that the vast majority of our population are not risk-takers. Gamblers are the ultimate risk-takers (along with extreme sports competitors) in my estimation. No matter what the odds are, a gambler will tell you that somebody somewhere, sometime always wins—and it just might be him or her. So they take the risk. What are the odds in second marriage/blended family risk-taking? The fact that more second marriages fail than first marriages doesn't seem to deter those anxious to blend their families and share their lives with each other. (I for one am glad for that every time I perform a blended family wedding.)

What are the unknowns in building a blended family? Everything, starting with the parental relationship. What if one parent or the other gives up when the going gets tough? What if your children never really like and get along with your mate's children? What if a former spouse decides to wage war on us and our family? What if we run out of money and spend all our time fighting the dollar war? Is your fear level climbing yet? Am I describing what you are currently living with but refuse to get help for? If you are still considering blending families, are you willing to risk the unknown?

There are two kinds of risk-taking. The first is where you do all your homework and learn everything you can before you take the risk. The second is where two people fall in love and hope everything else will fall into place. I am a strong proponent of the first kind of risk-taking. To minimize and defuse stress and differences, I recommend pre-second marriage/blended family counseling and testing. (Since there are numerous helpful tests on the market to help blended families work together better and communicate more effectively, I suggest you contact a Christian psychologist who works with family systems and see what he or she recommends.) If we are not willing to start there, we risk swimming with icebergs, and we just might hit one and sink. I am also a strong advocate of joining a blended family fellowship group in our church or community. We learn from each other far more than from the books we read or the workshops we attend on how to be a better blended family. The road map into blended family country is drawn daily by those taking the journey. They are the experts, survivors, navigators, guides. There are fewer unknowns if you stay close to those who know the way. I believe C.S. Lewis was right when he said the thing that draws us close to one another in our journey is "What! You, too? I thought I was the only one!"

Perhaps the greatest risk of the unknown in second marriage/blended families is wondering if those involved will change from what they are to something you may not like, understand, or want to continue spending the rest of your life with. Few people stay the same over time. And though some people seldom are unpredictable, others, for reasons known and unknown, change. And those changes often alter the family picture.

Am I scaring you with the realities of my experience? That is not my intention. I want to challenge you to be an intelligent risk-taker who always does his or her homework, grabs the hand of God with a firm grip, and lives with reality when preparing for or living in a blended family. Everyone comes to a blended family with a prior history of life somewhere else. The new family members risk moving into the unknown with you. Their new history is being built with you and your spouse each day. The gifts of *love* and *time* make the risk of the unknown less threatening.

4. Are you willing to risk self-discovery?

The Greek philosopher Socrates said "know thyself." Everything else he ever said or other great philosophers said pales in significance to this challenge. Few of us can say that we really do know ourselves. We know the obvious, the familiar, the things others tell us about ourselves. But real self-knowledge eludes us because we are too busy trying to figure out everything going on around us.

We really discover ourselves when we are in a safe environment that allows that to happen. If we don't feel safe and accepted, our human tendency is to keep our walls in place and our vulnerability hidden from view. A healthy blended family is one that allows everyone in it to discover who they really are, to have that affirmed and acknowledged, and to pursue further discovery as the years go by.

Along the trail in life, all of us have asked the questions, Who am I? How did I get here? Why am I here, and where am I going? The questions hit the wall and bounce back in our faces unanswered until we, through wise teaching and guidance, begin to understand that we are God's unique, unrepeatable miracles. We are gifted, and God has a plan for each of our lives.

I believe the hardest and most valuable gift that members of a blended family need to receive is that they are special and loved by God, even though they are living in the reconfiguration of a blended family. They need to be encouraged to grow in their relationship with God, with others, and with themselves.

Knowing who you were before you were in a blended family is important. Knowing who you are and how important you are in a blended family is vital to your growth and self-discovery. Over the years, I have talked to many children who live in blended families. Too many of them have told me they felt lost, unimportant, demeaned, unloved, and totally irrelevant to the ultimate destiny of their family unit. People don't discover who they really are in that kind of system.

I have asked many parent groups to sit down with their family units and ask their children, "Who do you feel you are in our family?" "Do you feel free to discover who you are in this family unit?" Parents have responded with surprise when their children expressed a sense of identity loss and lack of freedom to discover themselves.

I am a trained life coach, and life coaching teaches you to ask questions and *listen* to people's responses. I encourage you to start asking the questions and *really listen* to the responses. Too many family units, blended or not, specialize in "telling" rather than "asking." Telling elicits a yes or a no answer usually. Asking gives room for feelings, ideas, concerns, fears, and so forth, to be shared. Asking gives a person a chance to respond with honor and integrity.

Self-discovery starts with *asking* and is followed by *listening*.

5. Are you willing to be rejected and misunderstood?

"No and no," you are probably saying. You work long and hard at being accepted and understood. So do all the members of your blended family. So what's the problem?

The contagious disease of rejection is tightly woven into the fabric of our culture. We experience it in infancy, and it stays planted in our beings until we die. We work very hard to gain acceptance because it is far less painful to live with than rejection. From my ministry experience, I believe that one of the top-ten battles in a blended family is the battle for acceptance. The larger the family system, the greater the struggle for acceptance. "Human nature leads us to accept our own children over the children of others." If that's the credo in your blended family, it won't be long before those experiencing rejection sink the ship. Equality is one tough mountain to climb in the "your kids, my kids" battle. If you are unwilling to climb it, you should have stayed a single parent.

The excuse that it is too hard to be fair and equal with all the children doesn't ring true. When we say that the blended family comes with carrying charges, we mean *equal* carrying charges. Remember my growing up in a blended family story about inequality? I know how that felt, and I remember the tears that fell and the questions that never got answered.

When I asked whether you were prepared to be rejected and misunderstood, the implication was not that everyone in a blended family should expect and accept this as something that goes with the territory of blended family living. Tragically it often does, but that doesn't make it right. Your job as a parent is to work hard to prevent misunderstandings and feelings of rejection from damaging and destroying family members. When you see it happening, stomp on it!

I know children who have grown up in blended families. I have heard some of them tell me that it was a wonderful, loving, and growing experience, and it powerfully contributed to who they are today. I have also listened to sad stories of bad blended family experiences and the resulting bitterness.

A friend of mine recently said, "It's really hard to love someone else's kids, but it isn't impossible." I agree, especially with God's help.

1. In this chapter, what spoke the loudest to you?*

2. How do you plan to implement that in your life?

3. What difference do you feel that will make in your personal life or in the life of your blended family?

4. Who can you call on to help you and hold you accountable to bring that to reailty?

5. List three action steps you will take as a result of reading this chapter.

6. What key role will this chapter play in the long-term growth and development of your blended family?

TWO

Assuming
Personal Responsibility

H ER EYES WELLED UP WITH TEARS as she told me her
story. In a previous day's discussion with her spouse,
she tried to talk about each person doing his part to make
their blended family better. As the dialog veered out of
control, her husband screamed, "Don't tell me what my
kids should and should not be doing. Your kids aren't perfect, either." His parting shot prior to a loud door slam
was, "We'll do what we think we should, and you can do
anything you want!"

At issue in this oft-repeated exchange was the need for
all the players in this blended family system to take responsibility for the things they had previously agreed upon. The
system ruptured when those involved decided to drop their
responsibilities. When they were called to accountability, a
battle erupted when the husband decided to defend his
own children. The "us" versus "them" is one of the largest
sources of conflict in any blended family. Instead of a well-
negotiated truce that puts everyone on level ground, each
side adds a few more points (usually using negativity) to
their score. Without wise intervention and resolution, your

parenting solidarity will disappear, and the family unit will lurch out of control.

The father *and* mother in any blended family must assume equal responsibility when standards of personal responsibility are questioned or violated. The natural inclination in most children is to get out of any responsibility they can. Blended family children are no exception. They naturally expect to be defended and protected by their birth parent. If their personal responsibilities have changed dramatically from the primary family unit, they will find it easy to scream "It's not fair" at every turn in the road. I have told many blended family parents that they will live in the war zone forever unless they present a united parental front to all the children in their family. Many tell me they have talked about this, but never activated the principles to make it work.

May I suggest some team-building concepts that can dramatically change the way your blended family functions?

Team Blended Family

A few months ago, my wife and I visited the site of the 2002 Winter Olympics in Park City, Utah. One store in town was filled with apparel representing the different countries that competed in the Olympics. Many articles of clothing had TEAM USA or TEAM CANADA prominently placed in large letters. The idea seemed to be that you could be a member-come-lately of your country's Olympic team simply by buying and wearing their logo. You didn't have to compete, and you didn't have to be there in person during the events. You could buy the sweatshirt and declare your team allegiance.

What would happen if every member of a blended family wore a T-shirt with the lettering BLENDED FAMILY

TEAM on it? Would they automatically become responsible team members? Would they cheer for each other, work together, and accomplish great things? Would all differences end? Would the family become a powerhouse of team members who not only fulfilled their responsibilities but helped other family members with theirs?

Some of you are thinking "in your dreams," while the rest of you probably wish life-and-team building was that simple.

All of the front-line training programs in the corporate world today emphasize the power of team-building. The business community has realized that good management is not a "top down" but "bottom up" operation. Team-building always starts with the potential team players, not the leaders in corporate offices. If there are no teams who understand the power and importance of working as a team, all the solo efforts on the planet will never replace the strength of the team concept. Athletic teams understand this better than most people. The best batters on a baseball team will not win the World Series on individual strength alone. It takes a team and a strong team effort to win ball games.

How powerful would a blended family be if the team concept were presented and lived out as a way of life? A father and mother fulfill three roles in this team—players on the blended family team, along with other team members, coaches from time to time, and once in awhile referees, in the sense of reminding the team members what the agreed upon rules were when the game was started.

With every second marriage/blended family event, a new team is formed. They start out with rules from a former team often as part of their thinking. In order for this family to survive and grow, the old rules have to be forgotten and the new rules installed over time. Prayer and the universal acceptance of the new rules and responsibilities are mandates. This doesn't happen overnight. My experience says it will take a year of hard work—of failure, restarting, long conversations, and lots of cheerleading.

The power of a team is found in the personal support each team member gives to the others and receives from them. The stronger that support, the stronger the team becomes. The stronger the team, the happier and more productive the blended family becomes. It won't be long before your team wants to trade in their BLENDED FAMILY TEAM shirts for TEAM JONES or TEAM SMITH shirts (or whatever your family name is).

Wearing a shirt doesn't make you a team member. Being *on* the team makes you a team member. Remember, teamwork makes the dream work!

Miracle Teams

Miracle teams are teams that were not supposed to win and due to finish dead last in whatever sport they were competing. The USA hockey team that defeated the Russians for a gold medal in the Winter Olympics some years ago was tabbed a "miracle team." The New York Mets, when they won the World Series in 1969, was called a "miracle team." Sports history is filled with the stories of men and women on teams who were never thought of as contenders for a championship, but nevertheless attained top status. And you and I love it when a miracle team or a miracle person takes the top prize.

Last Sunday, I performed a wedding ceremony of two adults and five children that I feel have a shot at being a MIRACLE BLENDED FAMILY TEAM. They will never be crowned that on some nationally recognizable level, but in the world of successful blended families, they are strong candidates. Both adults had walked through painful divorces. Both struggled to maintain a healthy, single-parent family. All of their children went through the loss and woundedness of divorce with them. They struggled economically to survive and wondered privately if they would ever remarry.

After meeting each other, they took two years to talk, think, pray, and share with each other. They gave their children great latitude in spending time with each other and getting to really know each other.

At the end of the wedding ceremony, each parent made personal commitments to the other parent's children regarding their future lives together. I heard one of them say "I will always be there for you." What a powerful promise to make. The entire blended family was introduced to the wedding guests to the theme song from *The Brady Bunch*. As they marched around the auditorium, I genuinely felt that they were already a miracle in the making. What were some of the personal ingredients for this new blended family?

- the deep and loving personal commitment the parents have for each other
- both parents had allowed sufficient time for the wounds of their first marriage to heal
- the parents were in no hurry to get married
- their children had time to know each other and do things together
- they both went through premarital second marriage counseling and testing
- they both had a strong spiritual center and deep personal commitment to God

I believe those six things form the ingredients for any successful blended family and will put it into the category of "miracle blended family" stature. I have watched other blended families over the years put down the same foundation for their own miracles. Some have now been married more than ten years, and their miracle is alive and well.

What is the strongest thread that makes any blended family a *miracle* family? Becoming a team and realizing that their team is a winning team because each member wants to assume the personal responsibility to make that miracle happen.

Team Captains

At the very center of every athletic team there is a captain, or sometimes co-captains. This role usually falls to the most respected player(s), who can speak for the team when decisions need to be made both on and off the field of play. The captains are usually team motivators who can say the hard things that need to be said and call teammates to accountability when needed. The team leaders call for trust from team members and team fans alike. They are often not highly visible, but their presence is felt strongly throughout the organization. Perhaps most of all, they are listened to when they speak.

The role of father and mother often falls closely to that of team co-captains. They are expected to lead the blended family and have the respect of all the children involved. That role and the respect for it do not come by verbal mandate but by the hands-on experience over the long haul. I have watched too many mothers and fathers march into a blended family and demand the respect, obedience, and trust they have not earned. Consequently, they may never receive it.

Any leadership role starts by the leader being unafraid to tell those he is called to lead who he or she really is. That takes a great degree of honesty and vulnerability on the leader's part. I remember one father sitting down with his new blended family a week after his honeymoon trip and telling them clearly everything he could about himself and ending with the comment, "I have never done this kind of family before, and the only way I can do it now is with all of you giving me 100 percent of your help. I can't do this without your help!" Guess what kind of response he received? They all wanted to help him in any way they could because they were helping build the team.

There is an old saying, "People support what they help create." An open heart and an open spirit are an invitation for everyone to help create a new blended family. But remember, as a newly installed family co-captain, some of the players may decide that they would rather trade you to another team. They may reflect back to their primary team where everyone was a captain or no one was a captain and express their wish for "the good old days."

In my years of working with families, I can't recall too many blended family teams that just slipped into gear and lived happily ever after. One friend and potential co-captain described her early days in her blended family as "long depressing periods of resistance followed by shorter periods of resistance." Did she ever win captain status? Yes, but it was a long haul and hard work.

We live in a world of instantaneousness. If what we want is not instantly attainable, our tendency is to give up and go elsewhere. Dads and moms in blended families who commit to the long haul don't look for exit doors. They realize that tough times never last, but tough people do.

The essential ingredients that team co-captains in the blended family must stir through are:

1. understanding the importance of acceptance
2. actualizing commitments
3. working on communication
4. learning how to be consistent
5. setting disciplinary standards
6. being flexible
7. being impartial
8. exhibiting patience
9. building honest relationships
10. displaying humility and selflessness

You probably just took a deep breath and said, "If that's what it takes to be a captain, I just want to be the water boy or girl!" Lists of ideals are just that—lists. Very few people do lists, but we can take a few of the principles on the list that we most need to work on and get started. Most of the above things can be implemented with simple action steps.

1. love
2. hang in there
3. talk lots
4. stay on track
5. give guidelines
6. go with the flow
7. treat everyone alike
8. be cool
9. tell the truth
10. be a servant

Does this list seem more doable now? I hope so. When these things become the standard for co-captains in a blended family and are shared with love and exuberance, the entire unit benefits and grows. The order of importance *always* starts with *love*. Love is something you do! Jesus' great command to the disciples was to "love one another." Those marching orders have not changed.

Many children making the transition from a family shattered by divorce to a "new" family are inwardly wondering if they can be loved by this new father or mother. When they know they are loved, many other pieces of pain and hurt begin to disappear.

Just declaring that you and your spouse are the team captains, as I said earlier, doesn't make it happen. You have to want to be captains, starting at your heart level. It's not a fanfare position. It is one of honor and respect...and that's how good leaders lead.

The Wanna-Be Captains

He sat in my office on his lunch break and with his head in his hands said, "I can't do this anymore. I want out!" He was in his second year of a blended family experience. His birth children were grown and gone. His wife had a 17-year-old son who was living with them. As his story unfolded, it sounded like that old familiar line "the inmates are running the asylum."

His wife allowed her son free rein and granted her husband no authority over him whatever. Whenever the husband tried to intervene in any conflict involving the son, he was told to butt out by the son and told by his wife that she would handle the problem. Her idea of handling the problem was to let her son do whatever he wanted because he was her only child. Within weeks, a second divorce was in progress. Years later, this man was married to a woman with *no* children.

In the long list of things that destroy second marriage/blended families, the one right near the top of the list is the children. When children don't like the person their mother or father marries, they can tactfully place land mines that will eventually destroy the relationship. One mother recently told me she was hanging on by a thread waiting for a troublesome daughter to soon graduate from high school and move out. When I said, "That will be a celebration," she said, "No, that will be my life and marriage saver."

Many children in blended families are not out to destroy their parents' relationship but simply to take over the household and run it the way they want. I call them "wanna-be captains." As I listen to some blended family conflicts, I ask the parents, "Who is in charge here?" They usually stare at each other, shrug and say nothing—which tells me a great deal about who is running things.

I cannot emphasize enough the need for parents to present a unified front and take the captains' roles. When any form of mutiny is allowed, the ship is in great danger of sinking fast. If either parent lived a prior family life where the children called the shots, they are in danger of letting it happen again. This is one reason you need to take a lot of time talking about what you need to change from your former life that could endanger your current life. If we don't dump our baggage, we will take it with us into our current situations.

When a man and woman are building a relationship that could lead to a remarriage and the building of a blended family, I tell them to be a "Columbo" in their discussions. Ask the questions that need to be asked, scratch your head a couple of times, walk away, and think about what you heard. You will never do enough homework in this area. Once you are married, the homework you both did not do will never be made up. Although it's never too late to make changes, it will become more difficult with the passing of time. Remember, in a blended family, everything all goes into the blender unless you are smart enough to separate the good from the bad *before* the motor starts.

I believe most children want the happiness that a new family can bring for their parents and are not working overtime to destroy it. I have watched the happiness and smiles on kids' faces during a marriage ceremony. But I have also watched the anger on other kids' faces at wedding ceremonies. That ceremony usually sends the message to children that their original parents will not be getting back together again, and life for them will now forever be changed. That's not easy to swallow if their hope has been their primary parents' reunion. To some children, the wedding is the death of their hope, and it shows through their expression of loss. That feeling can hang around for a long time.

Teenagers, from my experience, have the most difficult time when their parents remarry and they have to join a blended family. They can be fiercely independent and diehard loyal to their former parent. They know they will soon be out on their own, but some work long and hard at making their statement of disapproval before they leave.

There is no room in a blended family for more than two co-captains. That mantle rests with the mother and father. It needs to be carefully guarded, otherwise some of the wanna-bes can quickly become the can-bes. Perseverance, love, prayer, and understanding are the keys to success.

1. In this chapter, what spoke the loudest to you?*

2. How do you plan to implement that in your life?

3. What difference do you feel that will make in your personal life or in the life of your blended family?

4. Who can you call on to help you and hold you accountable to bring that to reailty?

5. List three action steps you will take as a result of reading this chapter.

6. What key role will this chapter play in the long-term growth and development of your blended family?

THREE

Key 1:
Change

Facing the Inevitable Changes

Few things remain the same when you make the transition from a primary family to a single-parent family to a blended family. Within the space of two or three years, many people take those quantum leaps. Although I won't spend much time on it in this book, it's a huge leap to go from a two-parent family to becoming a single-parent family.

I am an avowed cheerleader for all single parents. I have been in their midst for more than 28 years, and I am still amazed and awed at how well they fulfill that challenge. All the job requirements of a primary family are still in place, but the work force has been cut in half and the economics usually follow close behind. Millions of men and women do single parenting every day and are successful at it.

When the transition is made from single parent to blended family parent, initially a sigh of relief comes from both adults. Finally, help has arrived and a team can be in harness again in their family structure. Everyone rejoices...

until they begin to face the inevitable changes that come. For some unknown reason, many new couples expect this new challenge to be a walk in the park on a sunny day. Their sheer optimism and the fact that they are in love with each other, they believe, should preclude any rain from falling on their parade. That attitude changes the first time a storm comes!

I don't want to give a list of changes that assume that everyone in a blended family has all of these things to contend with. Nor do I want to present some simplistic answers to each of them. I cannot know the individual dynamics in your family or your personalities. I will, however, offer a checklist in question form and ask how you are doing in that area. I can offer helpful suggestions at different points drawn from my professional experiences and hope they move you along in your blended family journey.

Where Are You Living? How Is That Working Out?

I have often been asked about the best living arrangement for a blended family. A place that is new to everyone is often best because no one has homestead rights. Everyone starts out with a new place and is on equal footing. It is tough to move into someone else's memory file where they have been the settlers for a long time. New family members can feel like very unwelcome visitors when that happens. If economics prevents that from happening, then redecorating and refurnishing can ease the new beginning process.

The ingredient of individual space is always a vital part of this equation. I believe all children need their own rooms. They need a door to close that shuts out some of life's intrusions. Everyone in a blended family needs some space that is his or hers exclusively. It is the one way we can all make the "world go away" when we need to.

They say in the real-estate world it's all about location, location, location when it comes to selling homes. I think the same is true in where a blended family lives. Are the schools good if the children have to change schools? Are the children close to former friends? Are they close to other family members, such as grandparents? Is the neighborhood a nourishing place or not? Will this place be like living in a foreign land for the blended family or will it seem like their homeland?

Too many times, the only question asked about housing is, "Can we afford it?" When a blended family is formed, housing can be a step up or a step down. When it's down, it is tough to swallow and family members can get lost in the "if I'd only" syndrome. That's why personal space is so important. Try to make everyone feel at home. One blended family that moved into different housing had an open house and invited their pastor to come and have a prayer of blessing over the new home. That's a great idea that you might want to do even if you have lived in your house a while.

A home means different things to each of us. It can be a powerful place of stability and a sanctuary for those who have lived through some unsettling times.

How Are the Family Relationships Working?

A remarriage/blended family creation usually makes strange things happen in the galaxy called family systems. It introduces myriad new planets into the world, and sometimes they bump into each other with very destructive force.

Your parent/grandparent system usually takes the first hit and sends debris in all directions. What do you do when your parents disapprove of your new relationship, let you know it, and tell you the "other children" will never be accepted as part of the extended family? What happens when grandparents decide the same thing? You cannot demand someone accept the people they don't want any part of. And, tragically, that often happens, and a wide rift comes to the blended family that may go on for years and never be resolved.

Fortunately most blended families gain wide acceptance from other members in their family system. Some extended family members are even overjoyed with the new happiness their relatives have found. I recently watched a grandfather in action at a blended family marriage event. He spent a great deal of time laughing, playing with, and hugging the new children joining his daughter's new family. I know that there was a year of acceptance and inclusion that started long before the wedding, which certainly had a positive impact. Bridges take time to build— and you build them *before* you need them. Too often expectations and explanations are not given time to be worked on by other family members prior to the marriage. Everyone needs time to work through their adjustments as well as their losses.

When my primary father was killed and my mother later chose to remarry, I was cut off from my real father's family. I knew growing up that I had a family of origin somewhere, but all the energies were given to connecting with the new family my stepfather brought with him. I was in my fifties when a strange set of circumstances got me back in touch with an entire family I did not know. My feelings ran the gamut from happiness to anger at my mother for not keeping in contact with my father's primary family. I felt deprived of all these wonderful people for so long. And yet I eventually realized it was no deliberate act on my mother's part that caused this to happen. Even though we were physically only 50 miles apart for many years, my mother had simply moved on with her life and left an entire family behind.

I have since watched that happen to many of the people I have worked with. Sometimes it is intentional, but often it happens because a blended family has already inherited another entire family and doesn't have enough time to envelop the whole family spectrum. Often your in-laws from your former marriage are who lose out. They find it hard to have a neutral place to stand, so they quietly disappear into the hedges and lose something valuable. My advice from my own experience is simple. Keep *all* the lines open, and work to keep valuable connections alive. And I am a strong believer in the effect and impact of grandparents on grandchildren. My advice is to stick as close to them as you can so your children can benefit. Work hard to help them know the new grandparents, if the grandparents are willing. You can never have too many grandparents!

Someone recently told me that they were heading back East soon for a family reunion. When I asked how often and how many would be coming, he said about 150 people, and they had the reunion every five years. I found myself a bit envious. He had a number of blended families in his family, but *all* were always invited, with no exclusions.

Divorce disrupts and dismembers family systems. Creating a blended family doesn't automatically heal those systems. Some parts of that system stay disconnected for years to come and nothing you can do, other than pray, can make a difference. I believe God created family for many good reasons, and everyone in a family system needs to work hard to keep the family alive. Fix what you can, stay away from what you can't fix, and have the wisdom to know the difference.

Who Handles the Money?

Only a few of us, myself not included, were taught good money management growing up. Maybe like me, you had to learn everything the hard way. When two people marry the first time, one of the primary issues and areas of conflict can be, and usually is, money management. When McFrugal marries McSpending, financial explosions are usually not far behind.

When two people marry for the second time, I am totally amazed at how little discussion there is about money management, indebtedness, planning, and saving. The carryover style, whether good or bad, is automatically inserted into the new family system. Unless the couple has experienced some good premarital second-marriage counseling, assumptions will rule the day, and the difficult discussions about money will be put on the back burner.

If the blended family comes with carrying charges, some of those carrying charges will be financial. If the new blended family father is paying child support to his children and also has the financial responsibility of his new wife's children, money can be very lean. Feelings of anger and resentment toward children you may not know well or may only see on weekend visitations can overwhelm a new spouse.

Until now, I have not drawn a line of distinction between the blended family that *all* lives together all the time in a little yellow house and the flip side, where the children of one spouse lives with the primary parent and only visits the little yellow house every other week, on special occasions, or in the summer. No matter who lives where when, when two people remarry and both have children, a blended family is created with complex financial arrangements.

Working on financial issues *prior* to building a blended family is wise and admirable. Once you are in the family, if you don't have a system that works and both parents agree upon, you need to get outside help fast. Many churches today are offering Crown Financial Ministries courses. The blended family members I have known who have taken these courses tell me they are eternally thankful, and that it ended the money wars. (You can find out more about Crown Financial Ministries at www.crown.org.)

In many blended families, the money management style of operation is "she has her money and checkbook, and I have my money and checkbook. She pays her bills, and I pay mine." For some people that seems to work, but I wonder if it's prompted by distrust or a control issue. Lots of things work, but the deeper question is "Am I happy with it or is there a better way?" The Christian teaching is that God owns everything, and you and I are to be good stewards in managing what he has given us. When that truth is foundational in a family system, we are well on the way to sound financial management.

Because people's gifts and talents lie in different areas, I believe the one who keeps the budget and pays the bills should be the one who enjoys doing that, has a talent for it, and can do it better than anyone else in the family. Sometimes pride gets in the way of our real talents. One father in a blended family insisted he take care of all the money management because the Bible said he was the head of the household. Yes, the Bible does say that, but it doesn't say the husband should always be the one to handle the money matters. He almost drove his family into bankruptcy because he did such a poor job at what he argued was "his" job. When he finally realized his wife was gifted in that area, she took over and saved them from financial disaster. In *every* family there is always one person more gifted at something than another person. When we can sit on our egos and let the best person for the job do the job, the good ship Family will sail on calmer seas. A well-planned family budget with the right person overseeing it relieves a lot of the financial tension that stresses out many blended families.

Do You Have a Healthy Discipline System?

I remember it like it happened yesterday. Every summer evening, a group of us met to play baseball on a grassy field near our homes. We worked on our farms all day and looked forward to the game at the end of the day. On this particular night, the game was well underway when one team member hit a long foul ball that he thought was fair. A loud and aggressive argument ensued, and when the majority declared the ball was foul, the batter who had hit the ball grabbed it from another player, got on his bicycle, and headed for home. No big deal—except it was the only ball we had to play with. Because he did not agree that his hit was inches into foul territory, he decided to make his own rule...*game over!*

Playing by the rules creates disagreements and arguments in every sport ever created. Since most sportspeople know the rules of their sport, they generally accept those rules and the umpire's enforcement of them, so that the game can be enjoyed by all participants. Everyone would agree that there would be no games without the rules that make them fair to everyone. In every family system on earth, there are some rules that enable the family to operate with order and a sense of fairness to all involved. Not all families and family members agree on what those rules should be and what disciplines should be enacted for those who break the rules.

We have all been rule-breakers sometime in our journey through life. Some have paid a great price for breaking the rules in their family system. Others have perfected a lifetime skill of breaking the rules and getting away with it. Most of us fall somewhere in between the penalized and the escapees.

When we create our first family system and our first child is born, rules start taking shape that will govern both that child's life and ours along with it. We read all the books that tell us what to do in various situations. We follow some and reject others. We absorb the disciplines our parents raised us with and incorporate them into our new family. We eventually come up with our own compilation of what works and what doesn't work, improvising as we go from year to year.

Some children are a joy to raise because they lovingly follow all our rules. Others rebel and bring the winds of chaos into our family system. Somehow, most of us survive, our children grow up, move out, and start their own families. That's the journey and the story for most primary families. For most blended families, that story takes more twists and turns before it ends.

When a new blended family is formed, disciplines and rules from the primary family of each spouse can collide. Rules of behavior that were once accepted and deeply ingrained in both the children and adults now are questioned, debated, abused, or abandoned. Each parent can add to the conflict by trying to enforce their former standards on the new spouse's children.

An added complication comes into play when children spend time on visits with their primary parents and a different set of rules and disciplines are in play. All it takes to terrorize a new blended family is for the primary parent to tell his or her children that they do not have to obey their new parent. I have watched continued conflict erupt when primary parents try to change the rules that their children now have to live under within their blended family. I watch the missiles being tossed over the weekend fence month after month. Nothing can cause more chaos in a blended family than an intruding former spouse.

How do we win this war? The only thing we can really do is tell our children what our disciplinary standards are and that they will be enforced in our household. We cannot control what happens when children are with a former spouse. There are myriad games that people still play in the post-divorce wars. Most of them focus on "getting even" with a former spouse.

Long before a blended family is formed, a father and mother need to talk long and hard about their beliefs in rules and disciplines for their children. Both need to be on the same page. If they are not, the addition of a former spouse also on another page will cause great conflict.

Family talk times about the "whys" of the disciplinary structure are important. Rules with no explanations are usually met with defiance and disobedience at every turn in the road. When possible, it is highly beneficial if a discussion can be held with a current spouse and former spouse so that *everyone* is on the same page. If that happens, it usually happens when all involved have allowed healing and forgiveness in their divorce. From my work experience, that is a down-the-road dream since most divorces are not amicable.

Disciplines and rules of behavior are boundaries that we need in our lives. We can only play the game if we know and follow the rules. In your family, posting the rules in plain sight on the refrigerator door is helpful. It lets family members know the rules are not just verbal and arbitrary. If there are variables for different children, they should have their own copies posted in their bedrooms.

There will always be an inherent tendency to favor one's own children over the "new additions" to your blended family. The personal guilt that a father or mother feels at having to drag their children through a messy divorce adds to that tendency. You will need to work hard to learn how to balance that out when it comes to discipline and family rules. Most children know where they fall in a family pecking system. Getting them to feel a sense of fairness and equality is a full-time but necessary job.

What Does Your Family's Spiritual Environment Look Like?

How is the spiritual aspect of your family? Seldom is that question ever asked in any family, primary or blended. The question is not "Do you go to church?" "Do you read the Bible?" "Do you pray?" A spiritual environment contains those elements, but it encompasses the *entire* home atmosphere along with the spiritual goals and objectives of every family member. Because we live in a consumer-driven culture, that consumer mentality has slipped into our religious and spiritual worlds. We tend to let people in spiritual roles set our spiritual environment by responding to their invitation to get involved in their spiritual programs. It is easy to believe our families are in a spiritual environment because they do all the things the church encourages them to do.

Am I anti church programs? No. In fact, I am definitely a strong church supporter. My concern is that parents make the church responsible for their family's spiritual environment and take no personal responsibility for forming and caring for it. Contemporary Christianity can be more spectator oriented than participant oriented. It is often easier to go and observe than to dig deep and instigate and support a family-oriented spiritual journey.

Over the years, my wife and I have gone on a few monastery retreats. We agree that one of the highlights of our time in a monastery facility is that we really feel we are in a spiritual environment. Monasteries are usually in out-of-the-way places and are very quiet, even at meal time. Visitors can attend different chapel services each day. They can spend time alone in the chapel, bookstore, or library in spiritual reading. Guests can observe the discipline of silence during their stay or talk to others. They can consult with a monastery brother or say nothing to any of them. There are no TVs or phones. The outside world seems far away when we stand on what I call "holy ground." Different spiritual icons and focus points mark the grounds. People can walk the stations of the cross, pray alone by a lake, or sing with the monks in chapel.

Have I lost you? Do you think I want to turn your home into a monastery? Not at all. I want you to envision what your family would look like if you were to make it more spiritually oriented. Maybe one room in your home could be a prayer room where family members could meet God alone in quiet. Perhaps some Christian symbols could be placed throughout your house. Christian music could be played more frequently. A prayer garden could be built in your backyard. When you add the outside ingredients that the church can offer to the inside ones you can create, your home environment will change.

Of course, your spouse needs to be an active participant in creating a spiritual atmosphere and attitude. And it's easier to get children interested if they are involved in planning and carrying out activities. Families need to creatively brainstorm and keep brainstorming ideas that will encourage biblical values and promote spirituality. People support what they help create.

Creating a healthy spiritual environment in your home also means doing spiritual things together. A family mission trip is a good place to start. Many churches offer that opportunity today, and it is great exposure to cross-cultural living for your family.

How Do You Make Memories and Traditions Important?

When a blended family is created, individuals come with past memories and traditions. These may be secretly tucked into the niches of people's past lives, but they are nevertheless there. They will live on in the new family and, from time to time, vie with new memories and traditions.

What do we do with the things people bring with them that we had no part in creating or participating in? The human tendency is to ignore them and pretend the new things we will create as a new family will far surpass the old memories and traditions. This is a big mistake that many in newly blended families make. Family albums, wedding pictures, and holiday traditions are vital parts of everyone's history. We can't deny the experiences and memories that other people have lived. They are the fabric of their lives. Packing them away in the dark recesses of our garages or attics doesn't make them disappear from people's minds. And some traditions from a prior family history need to be kept intact for the children. Scrapping them and adding all new is denying them of what they might hold valuable as a part of their history. The mental collectibles that people carry with them need to be honored and acknowledged. They need a rightful place along with the new things that are being formed. We can't remove what is imbedded in a person's brain, mind, or heart.

So what do we do with the memories? We keep them but file them in a safe place in our minds. And we open our hearts wide to all the new ones coming in. Creating new traditions is also vitally important. One very important tradition to celebrate each year is the anniversary of your marriage. Traditionally, husbands and wives do this without involving the children. Since they came with the establishment of this new family, I believe they need to be included in whatever celebration is planned. Traditional holidays should include something from each members past family tradition plus the adding of a new tradition that all have a hand in creating. When new traditions are created, *every* family member should have input and their suggestions taken seriously. (This excludes a surfing trip to Hawaii on each family member's birthday.) The newly blended family is a new chapter for everyone and needs to be memorialized. Activities done together will give us something to recall at our new family reunions.

Honor and respect what people bring with them into your blended family. Allow them to keep and hold important what they feel is precious to them. But also focus on creating new Kodak moments and traditions. Purposely look for opportunities to create memories.

How Strong Are Your Support Systems?

Within one year of a divorce, former husbands and wives can lose up to 90 percent of the friends they had when they were married. When a person loses a spouse by death, the friendship losses are still there, but the percentages are lower. The loss of friends shakes people's support systems and leaves them wandering around looking for people they can talk to and share their lives with. Many divorced people have told me that they feel like they have some communicable disease because former friends flee when they see them coming. The reality is that many people don't know what to say to those who are going through a painful experience. Instead of reaching out and asking how they can help, friends avoid the hurting person, and whatever relationship was there soon vanishes. Along with not knowing what to say, other former friends don't know what to do socially. Since couples tend to socialize around a couples format, the newly single person is an odd person out in a coupled world. A friend of mine emphasized how this impacted him by telling me that the only time he was invited to do something with former couples was when they had someone they wanted him to meet.

John Powell, in one of his books, says that one of our most basic human needs is the need to belong. From early childhood, we all look for those places, people, and things we can identify with and belong to in a significant way. I believe God created us to belong to an entity we call community. We find that in different forms and in different places and at different times. There is a sense of loneliness, emptiness, and fear when we don't have community. Building a support system and strong community is really a key to survival as a healthy human being. Support systems will change as we move through life, and vocations and geographics move us from place to place. Reaching out and making new connections and community can be difficult, but it's so important.

My wife and I have just moved a hundred miles away from our children and the people who have been community to us over the past eight years. We maybe know six people in our new area. It will be our responsibility to start connecting, and we will probably do that initially through finding a home church. Even after we find one, we have to work to know the people and invite them into our lives.

Back in my early years as a singles pastor, a few newly married couples who had created blended families asked me if they could start their own Sunday education class. Looking at our church list of adult classes, I suggested they join one already formed. After a few months, they reappeared in my office asking the same initial question. What happened? They found out they had little in common with married adults living in a primary family system. Their world was different, and they wanted to be with those who understood that and would build support systems with them.

One of the great services that singles groups, whether purely social or church related, provide is an opportunity to meet fellow travelers who have similar divorce experiences. In the past 20 years, churches have worked hard to provide this kind of support system to those who are uncoupled. Many churches have formed divorce support groups. That really helps people in divorce recovery because someone else understands what they have gone through in life.

Together we have and will experience similar things. Those things will bind us together in community. That doesn't mean this will be our only form of support. It will be the support foundation that we build on. Divorce support groups provide a relational anchor that gives a sense of security when problems and struggles arise. Other blended family members know the landscape, difficulties, hopes, and things that help better than anything else. We need them around us, and they need us around them.

Last Sunday, I was at a function with a large number of blended families present. They were part of a larger group of people of all ages. I noticed that the blended families congregated together at every opportunity, and I overheard them sharing blended family war stories. Lots of laughter poured out of the group as they talked and shared. I thought back some years to when most of those men and women walked into my divorce recovery seminar, broken, hurting, and in pain, wondering where their lives would go from there. For six weeks they formed small group communities supporting and hanging on to each other, hoping they would survive their divorces. That fledgling support system was their first lifeline of hope and recovery. The human need for that kind of lifeline never ends. The urgency of it may change from time to time, but the need remains.

If you are about to form a blended family or are already living in one, my question to you is simple: Do you have a strong support system that will help you do a better job as a blended family leader? If not, start to look for some blended families around you that you can link up with. Get to know the other adults in them. Plan some events where entire families can get to know each other. Form a support system where you can exchange the good and bad things that happen to you. Look for some other families that need what your group has to offer.

Is Your Former Spouse a Terrorist?

He was slowly coming unglued as he sat in my office and shared a too familiar story. His former spouse had just informed him she was taking him back to court for more support money. Along with that, she informed him that her children did not have to obey his new wife's house rules when at his house. He informed me that his former wife worked very hard at doing anything that would make his life miserable on a daily basis. He said, "How can she do those things? She is a terrorist!"

One of the top five deterrents to creating a happy blended family are former spouses who are not happy and do not want us to ever be happy. Like the flu, they hit us when we least expect it and make our lives just as miserable. The relief of getting final divorce papers and the oft-expressed comment "it's finally all over" means very little to ex-spouses who are just getting started at making our lives miserable.

The games that were played prior to divorce often continue and gather more steam as we emerge from the divorce tunnel. For many men and women, the retribution, retaliation, and revenge is revved up when a divorce is finalized and gains more momentum when a blended family is formed. As one woman recently remarked, "I know why that happens. They have a bigger target now!"

It is sad when people constantly seek personal revenge at the expense of making a new blended family a constant battle zone. For some that only subsides when a former spouse remarries and must then focus on building his or her own blended family. When that hasn't happened, excessive "get even" energy is like a guided missile aimed daily at the new family.

Disarming a terrorist-bent former spouse is daunting work. I believe the solution is having a battle plan we can enact when needed. How we respond is often a key to how former spouses will respond. The Bible says "a gentle answer turns away wrath" (Proverbs 15:1). In any and all conflicts, some of the answer is found in how we respond. As one seminar respondent recently said, "If they think they are getting to you, they will ramp up the attack. If they are not, they might just quit trying." Good advice. When we take away our former spouses' power, they quickly run out of gas.

Tragically, the target in some of these wars is not us but our new spouses. It is hard to see someone we love being a target of someone we once loved. Again, we, along with our spouses, need to have a plan as to how to handle those attacks. Gentle answer, no answer, silence…all work at different times.

Attacking through the children is the lowest blow. Children should *never* be used in any way to propagate conflict. They need to be allowed to have a healthy and honest relationship with both their blended family parents and their primary parents. At all costs, they should be exempt from adult conflicts.

Many blended families live an ongoing existence with constant destructive games played by former spouses. The conflicts of former lives often seep into our present lives and make it harder to have a happy home. If former spouses caused us heartache and unhappiness when we were married to them, the chances are good they will try to continue doing that. If they know they can get to us, they will. If they know they cannot get to us and pull our strings, the chances are they will stop trying. We set the boundaries, and we take control away from them. When they can't crash through the boundaries, they eventually get tired of trying and will bother someone else.

When we can achieve reasonably amicable relationships with former spouses on both sides and all parties can put their energies into making a healthy life for all the children involved, there is great reason to celebrate. This can and does happen, but it doesn't happen quickly or easily. Memories need to be put away, and hurts need to be healed. And that takes hard work.

Are You Living with a Family Plan?

"Do you want the family plan or the individual plan?" I don't know how many times I have been asked that question in my life. No matter what is being offered, the inquiring person is basically asking, "Are you alone in this or is it for you and your family unit?" When your children are little and still at home, if it's a dental or health plan...you want the family included. In later life, with children on their own (whatever that means), whatever plan is offered may be for you and your spouse or just you individually.

In the necessities of life, family plans are important. In creating and living out a blended family, an overall plan for the present and future of the family is vital. I am not talking about financial plans here, even though that is also important. I am talking about personal plans that involve every family member and the family as a unit for the years ahead.

Families make plans for various celebrations, vacations, graduations, and holidays, but if someone were to ask us if we had a plan for a blended family that involved every member in its planning and execution, I doubt that many would answer in the affirmative. If someone had asked me about my family plan when my children were growing up, I would have said for everyone to do well, be happy, and achieve success in life. Nothing was laid down in print as goals and objectives. We lived from day to day, as most families do, and hoped we would avoid major catastrophes and sicknesses and do well at everything we did. At the end of the month, we hoped we could pay our bills and have money left over for ice cream.

That may sound like a good and reasonable plan to you, but what we neglected to do was dream about our individual and collective futures, set goals as a family that involved everyone, and work to achieve that plan. We bounced around the country as I took various ministry jobs and hoped that each bounce would land us on the next rung of the ladder of upward mobility. Outwardly, it looked like we did okay. As I look back, though, I realize we did not live intentionally and with a workable game plan. We know that God worked in and through our lives, but I feel we did not use the brains he gave us for maximum family planning and achievement—both personal and for God's kingdom.

I have spent years listening to stories of what happened in people's lives. I have not spent very much time listening to the goals and plans people have for the rest of their lives. The reason? They are still letting life happen to them with no plan to take charge of what they want for themselves and their families. Some even spiritualize their situation and tell me God is in charge, and he will do whatever he wants in their lives so no plan is needed. The problem I have with that is that God has given us an intellect to use, and I believe he expects us to use it creatively and actively in dreaming and planning for our personal future and the future of our family members.

How do we start a family plan in our blended families? There are several things we can do. First, have a family dream session where individuals share their dreams for themselves and for their family. The next step is asking if the dreams are serious enough to transfer into goal status. Once a goal is established, someone has to take ownership of that goal and set down the steps that will make it happen. Accountability from *every* family member to help the other members reach their goals is next. No accountability and goals disappear. Goals of the family and goals of the individual members need to be printed out and posted where the people involved can see them on a daily basis. When a goal is achieved, cross it off the list and celebrate its accomplishment.

As children grow up, they tend to lean away from family and pursue their own interests and goals. If there are no family goals imbedded in their minds, they can drift away from their roots. A great family goal to form when the family is young is that no matter where all family members end up on the planet, once or twice a year everyone will get together for a few days. For instance, a friend of mine recently told me he was heading back East for his annual family week vacation on the ocean. The first week in July every year, all family members have pledged to come together. They all committed that no obstacle would stop that from happening. And this started in the way of a dream when they were all children.

Members of a blended family have usually all been wounded from the loss of a primary family. Dreams go out the door and futures are uncertain. Take the opportunity to help family members dream a new dream and see that attained because your family has a plan. Feel free to be creative in establishing family dreams and goals. It was the biblical leader Joshua who one day let his people know whom he would follow and serve. With boldness he said, "As for me and my household, we will serve the LORD." Perhaps the first plank in the platform of building a family plan ought to be that one, if it isn't already in place. Serving and following God in our plans demand creativity, dreaming, and a deep desire to emphasize the importance of family.

Does Your Family Have a Mission and Purpose?

The second and important link to having family dreams, goals, and plans is having a personal mission statement for your family and for each individual member. Mission statements became commonplace in the corporate world about 25 years ago. Corporate leaders began asking themselves the questions that often led to defining, in a few simple sentences, what they were in business to do. Their statements reflected who they were, what their purpose was, and the commitment they had to the world in marketing their product. The next step was to get every employee of that company to buy into and live out the mission statement.

Good mission statements keep a company on the course it was created to run on. When we can say with confidence, "This is who we are, and this is what we do," we will not wander into areas that are energy-sapping and put us in conflict with what we do best.

Mission statements are not sales slogans geared to sell products. Mission statements represent the higher road that a company travels on. I doubt you will ever find a mission statement of a major corporation that says, "Our reason for existing is to make all the money we can." That may be a subliminal bottom line that is never stated, but if pursued openly, it would drive both employees and consumers in another direction.

In many ways, a family is like a company or corporation in miniature. At its heart is a group of individuals who are diversely gifted and talented and should function with a strong team spirit and know what they do best as a unit. If someone asked, "What is the mission of your family?" what would you answer? You might laughingly say, "To love God, love each other, and have fun." There's nothing wrong with doing those things, but they are more general than specific. They are not rooted in the giftedness of members and the impact those collected gifts can make on the world.

When a family works to form its mission statement, many questions need to be asked. Why are we here? What are the unique gifts our family members combined have to offer? What words best describe our family? What do we want our family to be and do as a unit in the world today? What does our family want to be known for? What common goals can we unite around? What does the word mission mean to our family? Creating a mission statement that all can agree on and rally around takes time, maybe even months. But it's worth it!

A mission statement is a uniting force within a family. It's about *us* and not solely a *me* issue. When we talk about family as a team led by the co-captains, we are talking about the strength of a family. A mission statement is putting that strength into words that everyone can understand and be guided and motivated by. The individual members of a blended family usually have gone through enough disruptions to last a lifetime. Uniting family members can be greatly enhanced by forming a mission statement and living out that challenge. The next time someone asks "Who is the Jones family?" you can state your mission statement loudly and clearly.

What are some examples of mission statements? Jesus had one. In John 10:10 he said, "My purpose is to give life in all its fullness" (NLT). Everything he did reflected that. Many of the religious rulers around him were life-drainers. Jesus was a life-giver, and he pursued that through his healing ministry as well as in his teaching times. Even his parables were life-giving illustrations from agrarian examples.

My personal mission statement is "To be a shepherd, healer, and life coach to those God brings into my path." This is who I am, and how I am wired and gifted. Why would I want to work in an area of life that doesn't fit who I am? I have had some opportunities for those kind of distractions, but now I am able to run every opportunity through the grid of my mission statement, and I always ask, "Is that who I am?"

One of the best books I have come across for guidance in developing a mission statement is *The Path* by Laurie Beth Jones. In her book, she says there are three simple elements in developing a good mission statement. A mission statement should be no more than a single sentence long, it should be easily understood by a 12-year-old, and it should be able to be recited by memory at gunpoint. In other words, keep it simple, to the point, and don't forget it.

A mission statement is an action statement about who we are and what we are gifted to do. In some ways it will guide us in what to do in difficult situations. It will also help us to know what to say and how to act or respond in various situations. So read, explore, and talk about the mission of your family and each member's personal mission. Put into words what you can live out by actions in your blended family.

Sorrow Followed by Joy

When we lose a spouse by death or divorce, there is always a recovery process that follows that loss. The recovery process includes a period of time when we mourn and grieve. Even when the situation we left caused years of pain and struggle, we grieve the loss of "what might have been" but no longer will be.

Western culture, unlike many other cultures, wants to either deny the grief or get us through it in 24 hours so we can get on with our lives. There is seldom any thought given to a "time out" for mourning and there are very few standardized or ritualized processes we can follow. But people need to grieve when there's been a loss. The mourning process should allow time to think back and learn from where we have been on our journey. It should lock down the good memories and file away the bad. We need to think about what we have lost and why it was lost.

Mourning in biblical times carried the prescription of wearing sackcloth and being covered with ashes. Anyone approaching a person in mourning would give him or her wide berth, knowing that personal mourning was going on. In Western culture today, visible signs of mourning have been replaced by something not easily observed but far more troubling and difficult to deal with—depression.

We need to accept mourning as a natural process. It's a recognized sadness for the loss in a person's life. Mourning is a very private experience and has a different duration for different people. It is a time of recognized transition that prepares a person for the next step of closure in his or her life. Closure is not denying that the loss never happened; it is placing it in proper order in our lives and allowing it to remain there.

I have suggested that men and women take an inventory of losses, gains, and changes when they go through their mourning period. It doesn't matter if you are contemplating building a blended family or already living in one. It may even sound like outdated homework to some of you. But there is a great sense of relief in making peace with one's past and a willingness to count your blessings today. Based on my professional experience, here is a short list of losses and gains many divorced people experience.

> *Lost*...my primary family that I never planned to lose.
> *Gained*...a brand-new family and a whole new set of challenges.
>
> *Lost*...some friends and maybe a few family members.
> *Gained*...new friends and a new community.
>
> *Lost*...my spirit of independence.
> *Gained*...a new interdependence.
>
> *Lost*...my old church and its support.
> *Gained*...a new church family.
>
> *Lost*...my world as it was.
> *Gained*...a new world that is under construction.
>
> *Lost*...time I felt was wasted in my life.
> *Gained*...a time for redirection in my life.
>
> *Lost*...an old ending to many things.
> *Gained*...the chance for a new beginning.
>
> *Lost*...the time I spent looking for a new spouse.
> *Gained*...a new spouse.
>
> *Lost*...my private world of space and order.
> *Gained*...great people to share my space with.

Lost...trust.

Gained...the ability to trust again.

Lost...making decisions on my own.

Gained...sharing and making decisions together.

There are those moments in blended family living when we need to sit down and check our list of lost and gained. That is usually on the day when Murphy's Law has moved into your family with a vengeance and makes you wish you were alone on a desert island. We so easily forget what we went through to get to where we are. That's when we need to look at the positive aspects of our new lives. I grew up singing the song *Count Your Blessings*. One line says, "Count your many blessings, name them one by one, and it will surprise you what the Lord hath done." On the days when you find yourself looking for the exit sign, count your blessings. Focus on the things you have gained, ask God for the strength you need, and keep moving forward!

FOR DISCUSSION AND PERSONAL RESPONSE

1. In this chapter, what spoke the loudest to you?*

2. How do you plan to implement that in your life?

3. What difference do you feel that will make in your personal life or in the life of your blended family?

4. Who can you call on to help you and hold you accountable to bring that to reailty?

5. List three action steps you will take as a result of reading this chapter.

6. What key role will this chapter play in the long-term growth and development of your blended family?

4

Key 2:
Forgiveness

W E WERE ALMOST AT THE END of my weekly talk radio show. The topic for the day was forgiveness. The caller related a story about a long and bitter divorce and ended with the emphatic statement, "I will never forgive him for what he did to me." My co-host jumped in and asked the caller when her divorce happened. She almost yelled into the phone: "Twenty-five years ago, and I will never forgive him!" As the commercial came on, my friend and I both looked at each other with one of those "I don't believe it" looks. I drove home that day thinking about those long years of welled up anger and revenge that probably ran through that woman's mind. If her red-hot anger on this day had burned in her spirit every day for the past 25 years, I wondered about the tremendous waste of energy in this woman's life. It takes energy to stay angry and unforgiving. Unforgiveness is a fire that never dies of its own accord but will slowly sap your life from you and leave you empty and miserable and controlled by a bitter spirit.

I have met many of those angry and bitter people over my years of divorce recovery work. Most of them were venting their short-term anger and the desire to wreak havoc on their about-to-be former spouses. Our human nature, from very young childhood through adulthood, sends us seeking revenge when someone hurts us. You can be the most God-loving, spiritually mature Christian on the planet until someone targets your life with wrongdoing.

We want revenge at all the human injustices we watch on the evening news and read in the daily paper. We scream in our souls, "You can't get away with that!" and get even more riled when someone does get away with something. Anger, reprisal, and blame are a volatile mixture of combustible human emotions that can greatly damage both the person harboring them as well as the recipients to which they are directed. Emotions in a divorce situation can be just as strong. But Jesus knew and understood what stored up anger and resentment could do to the human spirit. When his disciples asked him to teach them how to pray, he said, "This, then, is how you should pray...'Forgive us our debts, as we also have forgiven our debtors'" (Matthew 6:9,12).

When the disciple Peter asked, "Lord, how many times shall I forgive my brother when he sins against me? Up to seven times?" Jesus answered, "I tell you, not seven times, but seventy-seven times" (Matthew 18:21,22). Jesus was saying that forgiveness is unlimited. I am sure that is not what the disciples wanted to hear. I am sure you and I don't want to hear that, either. We want a rule that says that after so many times, we can really let the people wronging us have it!

Perhaps the ultimate forgiveness saying came from Jesus on the cross at his crucifixion. He said, "Father, forgive them, for they do not know what they are doing" (Luke 23:34). In today's language, I believe Jesus was saying, "You can't live if you can't forgive!" Forgiveness is

God's detergent that washes the dirt out of our lives. It is also the glue that holds us together in human relationships. Without it, relationships fall apart and lives are not healed.

I've spoken of the need not to drag your emotional baggage from a former marriage into a new marriage. When you do, that baggage can destroy any current marriage or blended family. One of the biggest tools of destruction in excess baggage is the unwillingness to forgive your former spouse for anything that he or she did to end your marriage. If you can't forgive, you can't live a healthy existence anywhere with anyone. A lack of forgiveness gets in the way of building healthy relationships. It is like a poison or disease that afflicts everything in its path.

Dr. Fred Luskin, in his book *Forgive for Good*, says, "Know that forgiveness does not mean reconciliation or condoning an action. Your goals are peace and understanding, which come from focusing less on blaming, taking the life experience less personally, and changing your grievance story from a negative one to a positive one." Now that's a tall order for most people who have experienced deep hurts inflicted by another human being. The uncertainty about the response of another person to your forgiveness action has no guarantees. Forgiveness is always a risk, but what *you* risk if you are unforgiving is your mental and physical health.

In my divorce recovery workshops, I talk about the "forgiveness square." On the top of the square, I present an understanding of how God forgives us when we ask him to. On one side of the square, I teach the importance of self-forgiveness. Coming across the bottom, I talk about the importance of asking the other person to forgive *you* for whatever you might have done to contribute to the failure of your marriage. On the fourth side, I present the need for you to forgive when *you* are asked by your former spouse to forgive him or her. This is a great, teachable concept that works incredibly well when time, energy, and prayer are put into it. Working the forgiveness square is a key act that removes guilt in people's lives and allows them to move ahead with a lot less baggage. I don't believe a healthy blended family is possible when the new marriage partners have not dealt with the forgiveness issue.

I know it's hard to go back and take care of old homework assignments but unfinished business can be like pebbles in our shoes. We can still walk, but we will walk a lot better with the pebbles removed. I read an anonymous quote recently that supports the importance of forgiveness. It said, "Forgiveness frees the forgiver and the person who accepts forgiveness to live and to grow. It heals relationships and heals the spirit. It takes the sting out of memories that remain. Without forgiveness, there is resentment or guilt. Instead of human fellowship and release, there are separate prisons."

When forgiveness is not enacted, guilt takes over. Guilt, if not dealt with, can be one of the most destructive forces to infect a person's spirit. Guilt immobilizes people and causes them to live in fear. When fear grows, it destroys a person's ability to trust. When trust is gone, human relationships crumble. There is no more freeing and powerful concept than forgiveness. It is as important in your life and mine as water and oxygen. Unfortunately, we tend to fight against it more than utilize it. Pride and self-righteousness take over, and we want to exact a payment from the person who has hurt or wronged us. Even if we forgive, we want to add that closing line, "But I will never forget what you did to me."

Forgetting and forgiving are two vastly different principles. We are gifted with memories that pop up at the wrong time and remind us of things we would rather forget. Forgiving a person or asking for forgiveness is a process that wipes the slate clean. It is as if what happened really never happened. In a recent newspaper story, a man was convicted of raping a woman and spent many years in prison for that conviction. When the case was reopened, DNA proved the man did not commit the crime at all and was wrongly identified by the victim. When asked how he felt about the person who wrongly accused him and caused him to lose years from his life, he remarked with a smile for reporters, that he forgave the woman and held no ill feelings toward her. The woman even met him and joined in helping him rehabilitate his life. She became a caring friend to him. Could you do that? None of us really knows the answer until we are confronted by the situation. In follow-up stories, the former prisoner told interviewers that what he had learned in prison about God's love for him enabled him to practice forgiveness.

Dr. Arch Hart, a former professor at Fuller Seminary, said, "Forgiveness is surrendering my right to hurt you back if you hurt me." Are you willing to surrender that right and allow forgiveness to be God's detergent that washes pain, guilt, and fear out of your life? My challenge to you as a man or woman leading a blended family is simple and direct. Have you taken care of the forgiveness issues from your former marriage? Or are you still dragging them along behind you?

There are several helpful steps you can take in moving toward forgiveness. First, pray about the direction you need to take. Second, think about the enactment process. Should you do it in person, by letter, or email? From what you know about the other person, do you feel that he or she is in a place to understand and receive your intended message? Third, are there some key people who need to be in this process with you? Are they willing to help you? A pastor or Christian counselor can be valuable in helping you through this experience.

Always remember there are no guarantees when you enter the forgiveness process. I have had numerous people over the years tell me they did their part in the process but it was not received in a healing way by former spouses. The reality is that you cannot extract forgiveness from someone who is not willing to forgive. You are only responsible for *your* part of the process. Sometimes forgiveness from the other person comes later and sometimes not at all. Lift the part of the load you can from your shoulders and move on. That is all you can do.

I have found through my experiences as a friend and counselor to blended families, that the hope and prayer for amicable relationships with former spouses usually do not disappear over the horizon. They often continue because ex-spouses will weave in and out of our lives and our children's lives for years to come. It's better to be at peace than at war.

Have You Forgiven Your Current Spouse?

One deeply buried and often problematic issue in many blended families is the former life and existence of your current spouse and his or her family. In every blended family, there is a big chunk of your spouse's and his or her children's lives that you had no part of. When discussions of former life events and their relationships come up, it is very easy to become angry, jealous, and maybe even vindictive.

Steve was visibly upset when he stopped by my office on his lunch hour. His unfolding story took place at the dinner table the evening before. His stepchildren began telling stories of family vacations taken before Steve entered their lives. Happy and crazy times were remembered with a lot of laughter and even some side comments that those times no longer existed. A former family photograph album was even brought out to illustrate the experiences. Steve found himself becoming silent and sullen as the laughter and discussion intensified. Finally, he jumped up from the table and said, "That's the past, and you are not living there anymore." A deafening silence entered the room as he slammed the dining room door upon his exit.

This is a story too often repeated. Many blended families want to erase and banish all happy Kodak moments from the last marriage. When you did not help make the memory, you have no ownership of it. But all blended family members come from former lives with memories attached. They have a right to own them, keep them, and bring them into view from time to time. If you are a blended family father or mother, you need to set your children free to let their past invade their present from time to time.

We all know what not being included in something others had a great time being a part of feels like. May I offer a word of wisdom here? Celebrate the moment with them! Ask questions and let them know you are glad they were a part of that experience. They should not have to feel guilty and apologize for their former lives.

There is often a competitiveness that sets into the fiber of a new blended family. A new parent can work long and hard to make current experiences and memories far better than any past ones. It won't be long before everyone knows what game is being played. "Our family's better than your old family" becomes the battle cry. Don't go there! Creating a healthy blended family is not a competition with a former family that crumbled. Give everyone the right to have and express any thoughts—good and bad—from a former life. Their history is *not* your history—and that is okay. I suggested to Steve that he ask forgiveness for blowing his cool and, in his heart, forgive his new family for needing to remember and share their former lives. He said, "Hey, you are right. I just remembered I had a former life, too."

Forgiveness covers the waterfront on many of life's real issues. Not a day goes by that one doesn't have to exercise forgiveness. The adjustment to blended family living is huge for everyone involved. Hurtful things will be said at different times by everyone. The two toughest words in the English language, "I'm sorry," will echo through the blended family on a daily basis as the family members adjust their lives and lifestyles to the new challenge of becoming a TEAM BLENDED FAMILY.

Forgiving Your Family of Origin

Comedic and tragic movies and television shows portray the craziness that often resides in family systems. We all have tribal roots somewhere that we are proud to expose or ashamed to acknowledge. We have heard all the stories, and we have lived some of them. Families respond in different ways to the divorce or death of a family member. They respond to the remarriage and blended family creation by often pretending it did not happen and focus only on the man or woman family member who belongs to them.

When I conduct weddings that result in blended families, I always ask if the parents on both sides will be present.

Often the answer is no, followed by the reason that the family does not want to acknowledge this new union. Sisters and brothers, aunts and uncles, nephews and nieces may also become a part of the opposition team. I have seen too many tears at these events not to know that the hurts run deep and will probably never be healed. The sides people take and the issues that result sometimes defy logic and sane reasoning. Living out a divided family of origin can be a very lonely and painful experience.

Family wars started way back in the early pages of the Bible. By today's value judgments, we would probably call those families very dysfunctional. Many of those family members treated each other badly. And today it is no different. Some of my friends have told me that times like birthdays and special events have to be celebrated numerous times so that warring family members don't have to contend with each other and cause everyone to be miserable.

How do we live peacefully and with healthy attitudes in a war zone? I wish I could say do these five things and everything will be fine. But there isn't a set formula. I encourage people to look at their landscapes carefully, talk with their spouses and children, and form a plan that will enable them to walk over the coals. Don't let someone else's problem become our problem. We have to make decisions in the best interest of our families. The choices others make are theirs, and they have to live them out. I believe forgiveness plays a vital part here also. All of us have to forgive people who simply don't understand something and cause pain because of their lack of understanding and acceptance. When a man and woman take on the challenge of joining two families, they also accept the task of making wise and loving choices for that family. One blended family mother told me that their decisions were not up for vote by her primary family members. She prayed daily for divine guidance and kept moving ahead.

Forgiving those who don't agree with us is a challenge because they usually don't stop disagreeing, they seldom go away, and their vocal injections into our lives are hard to escape. Our best example of this was the way Jesus handled the religious rulers of his time. They constantly hounded him with questions and judgments, but he never let them deter him from his calling. He wasted little time with convincing arguments and debates.

Keeping Daily Records Clean

Winning something unexpected rates high on the good feeling list for most of us. I believe a close second to that is having someone forgive us for something that really hurt them personally. When that happens for most of us, we feel like we can fly. I believe God created us to respond fully to the things that exhilarate us and set us free from things that weigh us down. The choice to bear the weight or wash it away with forgiveness is ours. Most of us live so fast and so frantically that we seldom realize the hurts we inflict on others that linger without apology. Keeping our daily record clean in this area involves a renewed sensitivity to the feelings of others. What we say followed by what we do needs to be filtered through the lens of those in our own blended families. In the initial building of a new blended family, emotions often lie close to the surface. Feeling we are part of an eggshell-fragile existence is very common. Listening with the ears of our heart to what is said and what is felt will help us to know when a good injection of forgiveness is needed.

Blended family parents can be so consumed with their own adjustments to blended family living that they forget the needs and interplay of the children. If we are living obliviously to the heart sounds of our children, we need to ask them to forgive us for that. Our children should see forgiveness in action daily if they are to value it in their own lives. By modeling forgiveness we teach forgiveness. Children forgiving each other for misunderstandings, jealousy, conflict, and lack of love is important in our family dynamics. Children can be very insensitive at times to each other; in fact, they can be downright cruel. (Just visit any school playground and listen for 20 minutes.)

Forgiveness is a river that should flow through the life of *any* family. As fathers or mothers and team captains, we need to be the distributors of it as well as the beneficiaries.

Forgiving the Unkind Things Christians Say

Adults are not exempt from saying things that hurt one another. The escape clause we used as children, "sticks and stones may break my bones, but names will never hurt me," loses its strength in adulthood. We soon realize that things people say about us do hurt us. Fellow Christians, who often mean well, say very unkind things to us about people whose families break up in divorce. One of the most unkind things is to say, "If they were more spiritual, that would never have happened." Or that ultimate, all-time, guilt-inducing line, "Don't they know the Bible says divorce is wrong?" Most of the divorcing people I have worked with who have a church background have been nailed more than a few times with both those comments. I don't know too many people who were helped by negative judgments. Someone said, "The Christian army always shoots its wounded." Many who have been shot leave the church and sometimes drift away from their faith. When people need hope and healing, they won't spend a lot of time with those who indict and judge.

Coupled to those who add to the pain are those people who tell adults creating and living in blended families that God will not bless them because once divorced, people cannot remarry or they will be living in sin. That comment is not reserved for the pew warmers in churches. It can come like a knife wound from family members. It's very difficult for a family to build a spiritual center and strong faith when people close to them are condemning.

If this is the script you are currently living, what do you do? There was a time when I encouraged the recipients of these kinds of personal attacks to hang in there, pray, and let God work it out. I think I sacrificed a few people on that altar. Now I tell them to find a church that is loving, accepting, and healing—and to stay far away from those specializing in target practice on fellow Christians.

The positive thing we can do for those who don't understand is pray for them and practice forgiveness. Forgiving them is the first step in disabling them from causing us further pain. When we forgive, we put the offense behind us and move on. When we don't forgive, we keep the pain on the front burner of our lives and allow it to be destructive.

What Does It Mean to Forgive Yourself?

All forgiveness starts with God forgiving you and me. God's promise to do this is found in 1 John 1:9. The verse says, "If we confess our sins, he is faithful and just and will forgive us our sins and purify us from all unrighteousness." Confession is ownership of the wrongs we have done against God, others, and ourselves. The promise from God here is simple: We confess and He will forgive.

There isn't too much confession going on in our world today. Blaming has taken away the power of confession. We have bought into the belief system that says we don't have to take personal responsibility if we can find someone else to blame. Former President Harry S Truman was famous for the sign on his desk that said, "The buck stops here!" Today's sign would probably read, "The buck stops over there. I didn't do it!"

John Powell, writing in his book *Happiness Is an Inside Job,* says, "Blaming is a game. It removes me from reality. Blaming is essentially a way of shifting responsibility and maintaining power over others." When we assume responsibility for our lives and actions, we won't play the blame game. We will also find it easier to forgive ourselves for the wrong things we have done. No one does all the right things. Our human nature is mistake prone. We become healthier human beings when we understand that. When a mistake is made, to be healthy we admit it, ask forgiveness for it, and move on.

I watch many people specialize in beating themselves up over mistakes they have made. They talk about those mistakes incessantly, and the mistake grows bigger the more it is talked about. Their conversations tend to end with "If I'd only..." The truth is, "you did" and you have to make it right. Take ownership, confess, ask forgiveness, put it behind you, and move on. If God can forgive us when we sin and make mistakes, are you and I not called to do the same?

Are you up-to-date in forgiving yourself? I don't know what your particular issues are, but I do know that actualizing forgiveness in your life will set you free to live without guilt and self-condemnation. Someone has said, "Forget the past. There is no future in it." I agree with that, except that we can only forget it if we have dealt honestly with it. We cannot deny the things we did in our past that hurt us or hurt others. We can make those things right by taking forgiveness seriously and allowing it to be both a detergent and glue to the relationships we value in life.

The Power of Forgiveness

A few years ago, I was wrapping up a seminar and racing to catch a plane when a lady pushed a rumpled piece of paper into my hand and told me to read it when I had time. I pulled it out of my pocket as my plane took off and read the following:

> Forgiveness is a decision, not a feeling.
> Forgiveness is showing mercy even when you feel the injury was deliberate.
> Forgiveness is accepting the other person as he or she is.
> Forgiveness is taking a risk; it is making myself vulnerable.
> Forgiveness is accepting an apology.
> Forgiveness is choosing to love.

There was no author's name attributed to this writing. I have shared it in many divorce recovery workshops over the years because it summarizes the true power of forgiveness. Asking for and receiving forgiveness is a humbling experience. We all want to experience the end result even though we often wish we could escape the process.

Do you have some homework you need to do in this area? If so, I challenge you to pray, think, plan, and act. And don't forget—God is in the forgiveness business!

FOR DISCUSSION AND PERSONAL RESPONSE

1. In this chapter, what spoke the loudest to you?*

2. How do you plan to implement that in your life?

3. What difference do you feel that will make in your personal life or in the life of your blended family?

4. Who can you call on to help you and hold you accountable to bring that to reailty?

5. List three action steps you will take as a result of reading this chapter.

6. What key role will this chapter play in the long-term growth and development of your blended family?

FIVE

Key 3:
Communication

P AUL NEWMAN, IN THE FILM *Cool Hand Luke,* is hud-dled in the corner of a house blown apart by gunfire. As the deafening noise increases, Newman utters a classic film line, "What we have here is a failure to communicate!" How many times in a conversation have you felt a similar feeling? That there is a high degree of conversational noise going on, but there is no real communication happening? If someone were to stop you as you walked away and asked you what that conversation was all about, you probably would have said you had no idea.

We live in a world with more communication tech-nology than ever before. Cell phones and the internet have sent us into a free fall communicatively. We bounce back and forth from spectator to participant conversationally. When we are not doing the talking, the media talks to us. It is little wonder in our noise-filled world that no one really listens to what is being said anymore. People sounds have become just part of the landscape in our contemporary culture. We are so used to that backdrop of noise that we deliberately create sound when any part of our day becomes silent for even a minute.

Have you ever wondered if anyone listens to anyone else anymore? If verbal communication is a mandate for inter-personal relationships, is it any wonder that so many people in our culture suffer from acute loneliness? What happens in a family system where communication is poor or virtually nonexistent? What happens in a blended family when the barriers to meaningful communication are so mountainous that all the family members operate as Lone Rangers? Teams are built through effective communication by all the members of the team. No communication; no team. No team; no strong blended family. No strong blended family; a strong candidate for a second divorce.

Poor communication can kill or seriously harm a blended family. For example, the problems had been building in the Greens' new blended family for a number of months. The bigger the mound of family problems that needed to be dealt with, the less conversation there seemed to be. The father had come from a family of origin where problems were pushed into a corner and denied existence. His former marriage took on the same profile as his family of origin. A strong sense of denial seemed to make the problems disappear, but in the new blended family, unre-solved family problems only intensified the coming storm. The mother was the "let's talk it out" person. The more she pursued this path, the quieter and more withdrawn her husband became. The three children disappeared with their friends as much as possible to avoid the impending explosion. By the time the problem landed in my office, the big freeze was close to becoming a family meltdown.

I have watched far too many similar blended family struggles. In many family systems, there are those who want to deal with whatever realities land on their plate while there are opposing forces that specialize in deep denial. The end result is a standoff that can only be helped by the parents, in this case, learning how to honestly communicate with each other and form an agreed-upon plan for problem resolution. As I listened to the father, I found myself wishing for a 60-minute crash course in effective communication that I could give him.

Listen! Listen! Listen!

If you don't remember anything else from this chapter or this book, please remember that effective communication begins with listening. Few people do that well. Many people catch a few words here and there about what is being said, but their minds and hearts are somewhere else. I have been speaking to groups of people for more than 40 years. They look quiet and attentive for the most part, but if I were to stop and ask them to tell me what they were thinking about while I was talking, I would be fearful that many of them would be focused on something other than the information I was sharing.

Listening is something everyone needs to practice. It takes real mental effort to tune out both inward and outward sounds and focus solely on listening to the person communicating with us. To maintain and hold eye contact for some people is almost impossible. Some listeners want to look around at everything and anything else that is happening. They are fearful of missing out on something more important. When a person we are talking to keeps looking away, we have lost them and are wasting our time. When a person we are listening to keeps looking around the room as he talks, he will lose us. Insecure people usually have a hard time holding eye contact. Secure people can focus on the people they are listening to and make them feel that they are the most important people in the room. We all know when someone has really heard us. By listening to folks intently, we are saying they are important to us and what they want to say to us will be heard.

We all need to work hard at improving our listening skills. The war of distractions competes for our attention every minute of every day. When we don't listen well, we seldom get the whole picture, the whole need, or the whole problem. One of the most frequent comments I heard when I was in youth work was that teens' parents would never hear them out. I remember one teen stating, "No one ever listens to me in my family. I guess I'm not important enough." I am sure you would never want one of your children saying that to you!

When we focus our ability to listen without distraction, we really begin to hear what a person is saying from a heart level rather than only a head level. Counselors are trained to be active listeners. They know that if they are to really help a client, they need to hear the heart sounds. Effective counselors are long on listening and short on talking.

A way to build healthy communications in a blended family is to set up a ground rule that when things need to be talked about and dealt with, one person will be the listener for a stretch while the other person talks. Then the person listening will have the opportunity to talk and the other person listens. Before both people jump into a dialog and propose solutions to a situation, both will have had the opportunity to be heard without interruption. This works amazingly well in any communication setting whether parent to parent, parent to child, or child to child.

Setting the Stage for Effective Communication

Good communication does not take place in a room filled with a blaring television, a ringing telephone, a barking dog, a stereo going full blast in another room, and the dishwasher chugging away in the kitchen. People who are half-watching a television program while trying to have an important conversation should be duct-taped to the set for a week and denied food and water. Yes, watching TV when someone is trying to talk is one of *my* pet peeves! Is it important to create a good setting for an important conversation? Absolutely. My first rule for that to happen would be to turn off every sound-producing piece of technology. Refusing to be distracted by ringing telephones is a must—cell phones included. Comfortable seating and good lighting are also conducive to good communication. Add pen and paper for noting important things that are discussed, and you have the first step in setting the stage for effective communication. If the children are not needed in the conversation, they should be encouraged to leave for a time.

These few simple things will make vital communication incredibly more effective. They also emphasize the importance of the communication to all involved. When world leaders and politicians meet to discuss issues, they always set the stage and make the environment comfortable. Important topics deserve special preparations and settings.

If setting the stage for communication is critical, being personally prepared is also vital. How many important issues in a family discussion get side-tracked and go unresolved due to end-of-the-day fatigue and harried family schedules? Few of us do well when we are brain and body dead. A blended family will often have more schedule problems than a primary family has. They often have more players and more people to please. Good communication is essential to a smooth running blended family. Setting the guidelines to make that happen can begin even before the members become a family unit.

A Family Forum

In the flow of any family's life, everyone within that structure contributes to the big picture of family harmony or family distress. Having a regular or as-needed family forum gives everyone a chance to take ownership of the overall direction and game plan for the family. In a good family forum, complaints are listened to, talked out, and resolved. Schedules are coordinated, dreams are shared, heartaches are received, forgiveness is practiced, feelings are shared, and goals are affirmed. Does that sound like too big of an agenda?

I believe that having family forum times in a blended family is an important survival tool. The issues for resolution are usually more complex than in an original family. There are more voices of input trying to be heard, and there are oftentimes a few people who would like to see your blended family destroyed. As one woman reflected recently, "We don't have family forums in our blended family. We have war councils because it always seems like there is a war going on." I suggested they try to shift their communications to peace talks.

Who gets to participate in your family forums? Anyone who is even remotely part of the functioning of the family needs to be involved. Lest you wonder, no, not your former spouses—unless you have an amicable relationship with them and they are a part of an issue you are trying to resolve. When the adults involved in any divorce and the future building of a blended family are all committed to helping the children build the best life they can, things will run far more smoothly, and the children will be the beneficiaries.

Spouse-to-Spouse and Out of the House

There is a time in the life of every blended family that the mother and father will need to escape from the playing field and get some good R&R. Children can be auctioned off for the time you are gone to the highest bidder and talented entertainer. Just kidding, but you get my point. *Everyone* needs some time off to regroup and reconnect. In many blended families, both parents work, and the tiredness of working and running the complexities of a family can exhaust mind and spirit along with physical bodies. When burnout is just around the corner, it's time to get away for a day or two.

The away time is a good opportunity to review how things are going in your family. It is also time for a check on how each of you is personally doing. Feelings expressed need to be heard. Getting away removes people from the daily combat zone and gives them a better perspective on what needs to be done and how they can do it. For instance, over the years, I have done some of my best thinking on plane flights. At 36,000 feet, somehow things look different. All my distractions are down below and far removed from my line of vision. No one knows who I am or what I'm pondering. I have no decisions to make about where I am headed. The pilot makes those. I am removed from my world and can do nothing about it. It's a wonderful feeling!

Getting away periodically is renewing. It also provides an opportunity to talk about the things that require more time than we usually have at home. Heart-to-heart communication has a chance to get on the playing field of our lives. Time away together lets us grow closer when everyday life tends to pull us apart. Please understand that I am not talking about going on a church couples retreat. That's important, but it's a different experience.

There will be more reasons not to get away than to get away. Time and money constraints will loom as a deterrent. Your children will complain that they can't get on without you. And worst of all, you will probably tell yourself you don't deserve it. To all that, I say, *Get away anyway!* Do it when you need it, and keep doing it!

Do You Communicate Your Feelings?

The comedic skit I was watching on television featured a distraught man sitting in a therapist's office. As the man told his troubling story, the therapist would interrupt constantly with the question, "And how does that make you feel?" The skit ended with the frustrated man telling the therapist, "I need answers, not questions!" Most of us identify with the man who wanted to know how to solve his issues rather than being asked constantly to tell how everything made him feel. The truth is, we seldom tell anyone how we really feel about anything because we sense that the feelings we express will not change anything.

As humans, we have feelings about everything under the sun. We do one of two things with those feelings. We express them or repress them. Most of us do both at selected times. In spite of the comedy skit I mentioned, we all need a forum to express most of our feelings and to have them heard. It is more important to get them out and identify them than it is to repress them until one day they explode on someone in a harmful way. Communicating your feelings is vital to being a healthy human being. Feelings are neither right nor wrong. We get into trouble when we "act out" our feelings inappropriately, especially if someone gets hurt in the process. That's why it's important to deal with feelings as they occur, while they're not to the overwhelming, "I'm gonna blow" stage. We all need to take ownership of our feelings and, at the right times and right places, have the opportunity to express them in a safe forum.

In the divorce recovery workshops and blended family seminars I lead, I try to create a safe environment where participants can express their feelings. If someone says "I feel frustrated, sad, mad, or glad," that person is extending an invitation to others to know what is going on inside of him. He is also giving people the opportunity to offer some suggestions that might help him deal with those feelings in a positive way. One of the most powerful questions we can ask anyone is, "How do you feel about that?" If you ask that question, listen carefully for the answer and think about what you can offer to help.

Feelings abound in blended families. Many are repressed for fear of the consequences. But we can only lock away our feelings for a time before they spill out and our actions make them visible. If a teenager is mad at his dad and never expresses that feeling, he will only get more mad and the feeling will leak into other areas of his life. If members of the family feel like they are treated unfairly and don't make those feelings known, tensions will rise.

One of the greatest gifts members of a blended family can receive is the knowledge that they can always share their personal feelings and know that their place in the family will not be negatively affected by that admission. The freedom to think and share openly creates a safe place for family members.

If blended family members lived in a prior environment that was more secretive than free, it will be difficult for them to express their feelings openly. They may feel the new blended family is not a safe place. Old tapes die hard, and many blended family parents forget that. Weekend visits with a primary parent can place a child back in the old tape track. Children go through the hard process of adjusting to their new blended family all week long, only to have to readjust to a weekend family unit that operates differently. One teen described his situation as a "scrambled eggs existence."

To stay in touch with feelings is hard work. It is difficult to have the freedom to express those feelings. Being the recipient of the feelings of another person is also challenging. Sometimes shared feelings cause hurt, pain, and misunderstanding. The good news is that we can simply receive feelings and thank the person for his or her honesty and say that we will think about what they have said.

Sharing our feelings is truth-telling. Lying about our feelings pushes us further into hiding, and our backlog of hidden feelings gets larger. It doesn't matter if we are children or adults, the principle is the same.

Are you creating a safe place in your family where members can express their feelings openly? Do family members feel free to follow the biblical admonition to speak the truth in love?

Write Before You Speak

A spoken word cannot be retracted. Thoughts expressed verbally cannot be taken back or filed under "I never said that!" That's the main drawback with oral communication. Other factors that can interfere with effective communication are interruptions, emotional overload, defensiveness, and negative tone of voice. It's easy for our human emotions to get out of control in the verbal realm. Anger can instantly move in and derail the entire communication. And even when we've put a lot of thought into what we want to say—including practicing saying it without an audience first—the best rehearsed speeches once uttered may be misunderstood and misinterpreted. Once that's happened, an apology or attempted explanation of the words spoken will not erase the impact already made. What happens when we follow all the preparation rules and our communication hits a wall of resistance or interruption? We will probably say it didn't work and that continuing to try is hopeless. A barrier to further communication is erected, and we begin to let anger, hurt, pain, and rejection form scar tissue in our lives.

How can we avoid being misunderstood? How can we get our message across to the other person? Write it down! Writing takes the sting out of verbal venom. When we write important communication down, we can hone it and perfect it. We can work on it until all our thoughts are well said. Then we can mail it, email it, or hand it personally to the person we want to communicate with. When our thoughts are presented in written form, there are no rabbit trails to argue about or escape on. There are no verbal interruptions or arguments before we've finished our presentation. Now, some of you may think that sending written thoughts is a cowardly approach to communication. It isn't. In fact, it is a way of getting *all* your expressed thoughts received without verbal sparring.

Of course, there is no guarantee of amicable results because you chose this route. But you will have said everything you wanted to say in the way you wanted to say it.

You will be heard. You may get verbally thrashed in response or totally ignored, but you will have a sense of release at knowing your feelings were clearly communicated. But then again, after reading your thoughts, the person you're communicating with may understand what you're saying so well that a constructive dialog can take place.

I heartily recommend writing down your concerns when there are tough issues to communicate about. Sometimes just the act of writing down your thoughts can help you better understand the issues and perhaps reevaluate where you stand. The time it takes to jot down the facts also gives everyone an opportunity to calm down.

Encourage your family members to use this method. If appropriate, the written thoughts can be shared at family forums or on a one-on-one basis as needed.

Is there unfinished business you need to take care of right now through written communication?

Communicating the Most Needed Messages

The most wanted and needed message that everyone in your blended family needs to constantly hear is that he or she is loved by you, important to you, and needed by you. These are life-sustaining messages of affirmation. Without daily injections of affirmation, we die on the inside emotionally, and our self-worth and self-esteem becomes poor or nonexistent.

Divorce sends many negative and painful messages to those involved. The biggest and most injurious of all messages is to be told we are no longer loved. In my workshops, probably 70 percent of the men and women coming in the door have been the recipients of that message. Some received this message first in childhood when they were never, or very seldom, told they were loved. If that shoots your self-esteem apart in childhood, you won't have much to take with you into adulthood. When rejection hits you again via a divorce, you can be sidelined emotionally for a long time. The doubts that anyone will ever love you can powerfully impact your ability to be a healthy and growing person.

We are all in a lifetime quest to know that we are loved and important to other people. So much of what a blended family is about is replacing love that has been lost in the lives of both children and adults. Divorce often impacts children in the same way it affects adults. All parties can build walls to keep other people out of their lives so they can't be hurt again. Just saying the words "I love you" will not eradicate memories of being unloved. The words need to be reinforced by the *actions* of love on a daily basis. The rivers of hurt can be spanned by the bridges of love, but it will take time…lots of time.

Affirmation is the oxygen of our emotional existence. We need those daily reminders that we are valuable, gifted, loved, and important. I believe children in a blended family need to be overdosed in affirmation. They need to be touched and hugged all the time. If we are building a blended family, this is cornerstone material. We can have all the money and all the toys, but they will never replace love. Jesus knew this so well that his parting admonition to his disciples was to love one another.

Knowing that we are loved and important in our family doesn't make all the daily life struggles and differences disappear from our radar screen. But it does give us the security of knowing that when the problems come, the love will continue and never die.

Perhaps you need to make a sign to hang over the entrance to your home. That sign could read *Love Spoken*

Here. We all need constant reminders to keep us on track and call us back to the cornerstone of love.

Becoming a Great Communicator

Former President Ronald Reagan was known as the great communicator. For those of us listening to his speeches during his presidential reign, probably very few of us would have put him in that class. He was far from a thunderous orator that most of us would associate with a great communicator. His voice was very average, he didn't use words people didn't understand, and he seemed to talk like a farmer from small town USA most of the time. He seemed to communicate in neutral most of the time. His voice seldom betrayed inner emotions but was very calm and often gentle. I believe he was great because he was always simple enough to be understood, and his honesty and sincerity were seldom in question.

Unless you have belonged to Toastmasters or taken numerous speech classes, you probably don't consider yourself a great communicator. If you can't get anyone to do what you ask, you probably think you are a poor communicator. If your childhood was spent in a very noncommunicative family, you may doubt that you could ever be effective in human communication. Do all these things mean you should not try to be skilled in that area? No, it just means that you need to open the door to greater learning.

In the world of athletic coaching, you have everything from the screaming, criticizing, and the always loud coach to the quiet, arms folded, serene-looking coach who appears to be taking a siesta while his team is engaged in combat. Both types of coaches produce winning teams. The greater question might be, What does coaching style communicate to team members regarding exemplary living?

What I'm getting at is, What kind of communicating example are you setting as the father or mother to your children? The question is not whether they are getting *what* you are trying to communicate but rather what kind of communicator are you *modeling* before them?

Reviewing what I shared earlier, are you a listener first and a talker second? Are you an affirmer or a criticizer? Are you patient or impatient? Do you point out mistakes without offering help? Do you understand the blended family game and know how to coach it? These are only a few questions to help you look at your role as an effective communicator. Don't say you are not gifted in that role and don't want to do it. Instead, say you need help in improving in your role and are willing to learn and experiment.

The best question to ask children you are trying to communicate with is "Am I getting through to you?" If you have created a safe place for them to say no, then you can work on a better way to get them to understand.

Shoot for the Top Rung in Communicating

Those who teach communication skills tell us that there are five levels to all communication. On the bottom rung is what we call "cliché communications." This is identified as being superficial. When spoken in the form of a question or statement of well wishing, this level of speaking demands no particular response. The superficial cliché most common to our culture today is "Have a good day!"

At the second rung on the communications ladder is "fact reporting" or "statement making." This becomes the gossip level, where many people spend major amounts of time with little reward for their endeavor. Nothing is given of oneself, and nothing is expected in return. It would be comparable to reading the newspaper out loud from a park bench to those walking through the park.

The third rung involves "telling ideas, stories, and judgments." On this level, there is some communication of who we are, but it's not very personal. This process is usually more of a monologue than dialog. It really doesn't involve much of an audience. It is the kind of communication that permeates much of our culture today.

Our fourth rung involves the one-to-one "sharing of feelings and emotions." It could also involve one person sharing with a group. Recovery groups are focused on this level of communication. The first step into "gut level" dialog, it involves the risk of rejection if the other person or group cannot absorb, hear, or respond to what we are sharing. It also puts us into the danger zone for judgments to be formed by those who listen to us. Once we hang our emotions and feelings on the line, they are there for everyone to respond to. Once we go to the inside-out level, we are trusting those around us.

The top rung of communication is often called "peak communication." Absolute openness and honesty is maintained. All deep and authentic relationships are based on this level. When it happens, there is a feeling of mutual empathy and deep understanding, which takes relationships to the core of intimacy. Intimacy can be described as "sharing the deep truths of my life with others and receiving the deep truths they share with me"—and knowing that is where they will stay.

Most people will only have a small group of people who reside in their inner circle. Some gain access to that circle by suffering through similar situations in life. This is why recovery groups can be so successful. The empathy and identification is high, and trust grows well in the environment.

In a blended family, the goal should be peak communication. That takes a while to develop, and the other levels of communication will drift in and out. No one lives all the time on a mountaintop, but it doesn't mean we should quit climbing.

A quote I once heard could be valuable in keeping tabs on our growth in the communications area: "Big people talk about ideas, average people talk about things, and little people talk about other people." Talking about things and about people is a national pastime. We spend the vast majority of our verbal communications in that area. We add our comments and opinions to this sea of information, but not a lot of brain power is expended.

When we spend time communicating with others in the realm of ideas, our lives become incredibly creative, we are mentally stimulated, and anything can happen. Great inventions start by first giving birth to an idea. Sometimes ideas start by someone asking a question that no one has an answer for. As the question is kicked around, ideas begin to come to life. What would happen in your blended family if more time were spent on the creative process of talking about new ideas for your family? Anyone can report the facts of life and comment on them, but creative juices don't flow in that river.

Individuals in families have dreams that often go unexpressed for fear of being laughed at. In a family where ideas are welcomed and treated with seriousness, the family thrives and soon realizes there are no limitations to what they can accomplish both as a unit and individually. The fifth level, or idea level, is the "dream level" in communication. When dreams are not brought to life and die as a result, the person with the dream also dies.

Growing up in my blended family, I was never really encouraged to dream dreams that surpassed living on our farm. My world was very fenced in until I got away to college. It was there that ideas and creative thoughts got breathing room in my life. I began to meet idea people, and my life began to move out of my comfort zone and be challenged in a positive way. As I look back now, I realize how fortunate I have been to have idea people cross my path and keep nudging me forward to new horizons.

Have you ever looked at a family where everyone ended up being very successful in their chosen fields? How do you think that happened? Not by spending all their time talking about people and things while they were growing up. I suspect their parents were positive catalysts for ideas and dreams to be released and encouraged to take flight. As parents, you can be that to your children. You can create a new environment and a new level of communication that is both nourishing and challenging for your children and for you.

I believe there are two kinds of people in life...downers and lifters. The downers are the ones who say "You will never be able to do that." The lifters are the ones who say "Go for it. If you can dream it, you can do it!" Which environment do you think is the most conducive to launching people's dreams? Are you creating that environment in your family?

Using Coaching Principles as Communication Tools

My first job was in a hardware warehouse. My responsibility was to fill orders placed by our chain of stores. My first boss was a man who never told any of his crew what to do. He never gave orders; he asked questions. His favorite question was, "Can you help me do something?" Those of us in the order filling department would follow him around if things were slow, in hopes he would ask us to help him. Guys who eventually moved on to other jobs would always come back to visit Ralph when they had free time. He was a pretty simple man who knew how to motivate others by inviting them to help him.

Part of my time today is spent in life coaching. I work with individuals on a one-to-one basis to help them move their lives from where they are to where they want to be. I call them to accountability, I affirm them, and I keep them focused on what they are working on. I also ask them tons of questions because life coaching is built on asking the client the questions that will stimulate and challenge him or her to find the answers.

What would happen in your family if you started using that communication technique? Instead of telling them, ask them. You probably think I am coloring outside the lines here because you were taught that parenting involved telling the children what to do and when to do it. If they did what you told them, they were good kids. If they did not, they were branded as rebellious children. Some children can be told what to do and they do it. Others will not.

A typical family scenario happens at report-card time. The card is reviewed by each parent, and the two Ds stand out vividly. One question is usually asked: "How could you let this happen?" No reply is expected, but a number of "to do's" is presented in rapid succession. After the child has been thoroughly told, the conversation ends.

What would happen if you asked questions? Is this a tough subject for you? Do you understand the teacher? Is there some way we can help you get these grades up? How do you feel about the grades? What would you like to do to get the grades up? Questions give a person—adult and child—level ground to stand on. Questions don't threaten or knock people off kilter. They present options rather than give directions. They place the responsibility back on the child in a gentle way. Humiliation is traded for affirmation and encouragement. A great parent is not a marine drill sergeant but a coach. The Sarge commands and tells, while the parent-coach asks and affirms.

Who asks you and me the tough questions in our lives? Probably very few people because we feel it's not nice to be nosy and challenging. So we plod along, not even asking ourselves the tough questions. Life is really lived at the place of great questions that we are left to wrestle with and find an answer to. Even Jesus spent a great deal of time asking questions that his hearers were left to answer.

I want to challenge you as a mother or father in a blended family to switch gears from telling to asking some of the time. If no answer comes back from your question, let that be okay. Children need time to think through the questions and then respond. One of the apostle Paul's great challenges in one of his letters to the early church was "think on these things." We would all benefit greatly if we followed his challenge.

A parent in a blended family is many things. Team leader, captain, communicator, and coach. You will move from one to the other when called upon in your family. Each role helps you bring what is needed in different situations.

1. In this chapter, what spoke the loudest to you?*

2. How do you plan to implement that in your life?

3. What difference do you feel that will make in your personal life or in the life of your blended family?

4. Who can you call on to help you and hold you accountable to bring that to reailty?

5. List three action steps you will take as a result of reading this chapter.

6. What key role will this chapter play in the long-term growth and development of your blended family?

6
SIX

Key 4:
Compromise

MANY OF THE BLACK-AND-WHITE realities of a first marriage turn to assorted shades of gray in a second marriage/blended family. What was once plain and simple suddenly becomes very complex and intricate. Things once set in cement now float freely on the blended family pond. If survival and growth are to flourish, the fine art of compromise needs to be practiced.

In a first marriage, some people always seemed to get their own way when important decisions were made. Some spouses were passive and some were aggressive, adding to the first marriage dynamic. When a second marriage/ blended family is formed, the participants quickly find out that the new dynamics are far more complex than the old ones. Where the lines of control were formerly established and boundaries set, compromise now invades the scene. Compromise can involve any and all of the blending ingredients in a second marriage, from financial management to child-raising issues, from lifestyles to personal habits. Some of the most battle-scarred terrain in a blended family lies in the area of learning to compromise. Unless there is a warm environment of healthy give-and-take in the new family, constant combat will cause the family to self-destruct.

Compromise demands a great deal of work, understanding, and adjustment. Because most family members live with their own agendas, desires, and needs, the new blended family can become a real testing ground to see who will gain control and come out on top. Oftentimes the competition is parents versus children or one parent versus the other parent, with the children split in who they want in control.

The ability to compromise in the business world often decides whether a corporation will succeed or fail. The term "win–win" came out of the business community. It meant that through the art of compromise, everyone walks away a winner. There are no losers. That may be idealism at its shining best, but when everyone is a winner, everyone is happier.

Compromise is learning to negotiate difficult issues. I believe the heart of unity in any blended family lies in the ability of its members to practice the discipline of compromise. Yes, I said discipline, because that is exactly what it is and what it demands. In a compromise, we have to be willing to not get our own way and defer to others who may get their way. That's why it's crucial to make sure our potential partners understand and practice compromise. If we are control freaks, compromise will indeed be foreign territory. But it's a land that needs to be explored and lived in.

Ann's story is tinged with the sadness that surrounds the failure of a second marriage. She had waited a long time to remarry and blend her family with the man she was in love with. In the year previous to the marriage, Ann talked to me about a few red flags that were being raised in their relationship. She felt her about-to-be spouse had a tendency to control her life and decisions, but she wrote if off, feeling that things would change once they were married. And did they ever change. If her man was moderately controlling before the marriage, his need to dominate went out of control once the honeymoon was over. It got so bad that her children were afraid to come home from school at night.

Ann's husband didn't get compromise. So Ann tried counseling, but he tried to control the counselor. She tried having friends intervene but with no good results. The more she tried to work on the problem, the worse he became. Within a year of their wedding day, she and her children moved out and a divorce followed. What you see before you marry someone will not go away after you marry that person. Compromise is an art. It can be learned, but only if the person is interested in sharing responsibilities and control. Be careful! And if you are currently living with a person who is leaving controlling footprints all over your life, try to get help before the situation goes beyond help. Family violence is often the result of a controlling person out of control.

People with a need to control other people are not good marriage candidates and certainly will not lead in being willing to compromise on family issues as well as personal issues.

Nothing will destroy a blended family quicker. The flip side is also true. Compromise will strengthen family relationships, teach cooperation, and open the door for positive communication.

The Gentle Art of Compromise

I am sure there is a book out there somewhere that will give you 25 steps to the art of compromise. I don't have those steps, but I do know that one of the best compromise outcomes is when we give something of ourselves, and it results in a positive gain to another person. An example could be having a planned golf game for Saturdays when you receive a call asking if you can join a church work party for the day to fix some things on the church campus. Your compromise would be giving up the golf game. Your gain would be making the church facility a better place for all.

Most of us were born selfish. The first word many children learn after Mama and Dada is *mine!* Unless our parents teach the principle of sharing, we can go through life yelling *mine* and grab everything we can. For the person afflicted with a "mine attitude," it is very difficult to shift into a share and compromise mode. Sharing is all about servanthood, and very few (if any) are born with a desire to serve.

Teaching compromise in a blended family starts with reviewing the tapes that are playing in everyone's mind from former family situations. All members of a blended family come with their tapes going full speed. The model of life as they've experienced it is often how they want to continue to live. When adjustments have to be made to that model, there is a great challenge that won't be solved overnight. Children look to parents for an example to follow. And you'll have plenty of opportunities to show compromise as it enters into weekly family schedules, schools schedules, special events, work, household duties, visitation with parents of origin, finances, lifestyles, housing, room assignments, disciplines, and with primary family relatives. Toss in sports for a little flavoring, and you may be looking at negotiations every day for the rest of your life. But don't despair. When you have family members who are trying to live a life of faith in following God and what the Bible teaches, you should find it easier to come to the table when a compromise is needed. We serve God best when we are willing to serve each other.

For some family members, it will be a long and difficult journey from mine to not mine. If the family is going on a camping trip for vacation and you want to go somewhere else, it will be difficult to compromise without reminding your family how miserable you are every day. When you compromise, you leave your decision behind you and work at enjoying what you had no plan to do.

There will be no awards given to the parent who is the most compromising on issues in their family. You will know in your heart that what you did was the right thing to do. And you honor God when you put the needs of others before your own in a healthy, balanced way.

Compromising Your Expectations

Expectations are often built upon assumptions that are not connected to reality. We have expectations of every person in our lives and of every situation we encounter. We are built up or let down by fulfilled or nonfulfilled expectations.

The most basic expectation in every marriage is to live happily ever after. The love that creates the initial happiness between two people is expected to grow as the days, months, and years go by. People who are in love expect to be happy. When that surface love begins to fade, the happiness is diminished and the expectations fall by the wayside. Disappointments begin to take root, and a marriage can begin to falter. If constructive attempts to turn the marriage around are not made, divorce becomes inevitable.

There is nothing wrong with having high expectations for your marriage and your life. What can be wrong is believing they come about by an unknown mystical process. To live happily ever after is to work long and hard at the process. This is as true in a second marriage/blended family as in a first marriage.

When a first marriage ends, all your expectations go down the drain. If you marry again and create a blended family, how do you realistically form solid expectations you can live out in this new relationship? One of the wisest things to do is articulate your expectations prior to and early on in your new family. Whether great or small, outrageous or feasible, your expectations need to see the light of this new day and be heard by both your spouse and your children.

In the creation of a new blended family, new expectations are often formed atop the ashes of old ones that were never fulfilled in your first marriage. It is easy to compile a long list of what did not happen in a prior marriage and expect them all to happen overnight in your newly created family. Hope often lies in the new spouse doing what the ex-spouse did not do—fulfill your expectations.

One of the saddest stories I ever heard involved the mother of a young son whose former spouse had nothing further to do with their child after their divorce. She began a search for a new father for the child. She wanted him to be all the things the first father was not. After several years, she married a man who seemed to love and care deeply for the child during their dating days. However, once married, her new spouse clearly told her that she should ask her mother to raise the child so that the two of them could have the freedom to do what they wanted without any encumbrances. Needless to say, this marriage ended quickly. Obviously they needed to clarify their expectations.

Hiding the expectations we have of another person is often a way to avoid disappointments if those expectations are not fulfilled. We can play a game that says since they did not know, they are not at fault. However, this mind mechanics seldom decreases our frustration and disappointment in the person. The negative emotions still exist.

Hidden and unexpressed expectations can kill the spirits of both people. One doesn't know and can't therefore try, the other knows and is disappointed. Both are lost in the fog of hidden agendas.

Sometimes expectations are not shared for fear the other person will be overwhelmed by them and escape through the nearest exit door. If they are not shared and a new family is formed, there is always the danger that being truthful can cause both people to go into hiding emotionally. If love engenders happiness, then love also should mean letting go of fear. Expectations must always come out of hiding if the relationship is to thrive. They must be verbalized, discussed, understood, and lived out. The ones that are not in a reality zone should be discarded. Realistic ones should be formed into goals that both parties can work toward.

To help you understand what I am talking about, I want to give you two lists garnered from my ministry experiences. The first one is comprised of unrealistic expectations. Check how many of these are on your realistic list—but really don't belong there.

1. My new spouse will make me far happier than my former spouse.

2. My new spouse will be totally different from my former spouse.

3. My new spouse will always understand me.

4. My new spouse will have none of the bad habits of my former spouse.

5. My new spouse will be a better parent than my former spouse.

6. My new spouse will never disappoint me.

7. My new spouse will never handle money as poorly as my former spouse.

8. My new spouse will make me a better person.

9. My new spouse will make the pain and hurt from my first marriage disappear.

10. My new spouse is perfect!

If you knew that your new spouse thought these things about you, how would you feel? If you make these your expectations of your new spouse without the opportunity of compromise entering in, you are imposing impossible expectations on your new mate, and you will be deeply disappointed. Even though some of your expectations will remain private and subliminal, they will still stand between you and your spouse.

My second list contains *realistic* expectations that can be shared with your about-to-be or already-am blended family spouse.

1. My new spouse is not responsible for my happiness, but will contribute greatly to it.

2. My new spouse will not always understand me, because I don't always understand me.

3. My new spouse has a character and personality that was formed before I appeared on the scene. I will love and accept him or her.

4. My new spouse will have his or her own areas of struggle. I will try to understand and accept that.

5. My new spouse will have different styles of child discipline and management from mine. I will not

expect my partner to agree with and adapt to my styles, but I will work to blend both together for the good of the children.

6. My new spouse will not be the instant relief I need to put my first marriage to rest. He or she can only help in my healing. It is not his or her responsibility to make me whole and well.

7. My new spouse will be no more perfect than I am.

8. My new spouse will do things that will cause me to be disappointed. I accept that because we both are human. I will practice forgiveness.

9. My new spouse will love me, but sometimes in ways I don't expect.

10. I expect my new spouse to love my children as much as I love his or her children.

What would you like to add to this list? Are these things practical and workable in your new spouse relationship? Are some of these things homework for you both to talk through? This is a great way to introduce your ability to compromise and be truthful with the first list and to actualize the realistic things on the second list.

Lest we forget, a blended family consists of a father and a mother followed by a very diverse group of people called children. And whether you believe it or not, you have unrealistic as well as realistic expectations regarding them when entering into a blended family.

Let's look first at the unrealistic expectations we have for our children in this blending.

1. Blending two families is a snap and just needs a little organization.

2. We will all be one big, happy, contented "Brady Bunch."

3. The children will all love each other at first sight.

4. They will understand new parents, new rules, and new living quarters immediately.

5. They will simply adore and even mildly worship their new stepparent.

6. With a little discipline, they will all act, live, and think like the children in the *Sound of Music*.

7. They will be happier than ever before.

8. They will never fight with siblings from the "other" family.

9. They will respect the fact that money is short sometimes or at all times.

10. They will forever be thankful for this new blended family.

Some of you are reflecting on your new family and thinking, "Where did he get those things from?" From spending the last 28 years around blended families and their children.

On to the reality side, which should give you more hope.

1. You will spend a great deal of time patching the wounds of fragmented family members.

2. You will dread that part of the holidays when children pass each other in airports.

3. You will have more spare toys, blankets, towels, and sleeping bags in your home than you know what to do with.

4. Some days you will wonder what children belong to what parent on what planet.

5. You will quickly tire of being the "bad guy" step-parent.

6. You want all children to become wards of the court when it comes to dispensing discipline.

7. You will distinctly tire of hearing children say, "My real father (mother) said I could."

8. You will be loved and unloved all in the same minute some days.

9. You will expect God to give all stepparents a castle free of kids in heaven.

10. You will cry your eyes out when a stepson or step-daughter gets married.

11. You will never be free of your spouse's former spouse.

12. You may forever be going back to court.

Do you want to add a few of your own to this list? Some you can smile at, and some you can cry at.

Living in a blended family is getting your expectations out in the open and being willing to compromise. It is having expectations you can plan for and work on, and knowing that when they are not met, it isn't the end of the world. Expectations tied to reality with the ability to compromise can make your blended family a great experience.

The Ultimate Compromise...Blending the Ingredients

"Lifestyle" is a word that almost defies description. It involves hundreds, perhaps thousands, of little things that combine to describe how any one of us lives in today's culture. These are the things we have spent years collecting in our lives. Some are habitually ingrained in us, like which shoe we always put on first, exactly how we attack cleaning our teeth, the kinds of food we always buy, or the many ways we respond to the things that happen to us. Our lifestyle involves attitudes, personalities, mechanics, inherited traits, and a very long list of idiosyncrasies that are unique to who we are. We are a complex collection of life experiences. The longer we live, the more we add to that collection.

The people whose lifestyles most closely resemble our own usually are the ones around whom we build our support systems. Because they are most like us, they make us feel comfortable and safe. The people who are most unlike us make us feel uncertain and insecure. We all work hard at building our security around our particular lifestyle.

When two adults choose to create a blended family, their individual lifestyles will either collide or merge. If they have done their homework prior to establishing their new family, the chances are good that they have talked through how to compromise on different issues so that their families merge rather than crash into each other.

A second marriage/blended family creation can easily have two people who were married to their former spouses for 20 years or more. If they are in their early forties, they bring 80 years of life experience into this new relationship. They have formed their existent lifestyles, and now they are bringing them into an entirely new family system.

Who they are and who their own children are will take on a whole new identity and a whole new lifestyle. Compromises will need to be made on many fronts for this family merger to succeed.

Perhaps the greatest deterrent to the blending of two differing adult lifestyles is impatience. Along with the human part come two former marriage histories that will converge into this new family unit. If those past marriage histories still fall into the category of "current events" when they should be filed under "past experiences learned from" category, they will add an incendiary ingredient to the new blended family.

When I asked Gloria how her new blended family was working out, she responded with "Great. My husband and I are so compatible it's like we were raised in the same family." The issue of compatibility for the two adults in a blended family is usually high. Compatibility usually means we agree on almost everything. No differences, no arguments. Just plain compatible! From my experience, totally compatible lifestyles are rare. Many people go in search of a compatible mate only to find out that is a far from realistic goal. Even exceptional compatibility demands adjustments and the willingness to compromise.

One of the reasons I recommend premarital counseling in second marriages is to help the couple really find out what they have and do not have in common. I am a fan of the Myers-Briggs test. It is based on the book *Please Understand Me*, by David Kiersey and Marilyn Bates. The test points out the differences in a person, but also lets him or her know the compromises that will have to be made for a successful second marriage/blended family. This test is administered by psychologists and counselors specializing in family therapy. It is fun to take, and you will learn a lot about each other that you perhaps did not know.

Our human plea is that we all want to be understood. We have to know the other people well in order to understand them. Hence my cardinal remarriage rule: We should date a person at least a year before we consider marriage. Why? Because we need to see them through the many things a year exposes them to. And we need to watch closely what we see. When those red flags I mentioned earlier start flapping in the breeze, step back and ask yourself what is really going on.

One of the most enduring struggles in a blended family happens when a neat person marries a sloppy person. Very few people have the patience to put up with someone who is not on their organizational wavelength. People who live in the midst of constant debris don't understand why other people need perfectionism and organization. The opposite is also true. There are many rude awakenings during the first six months of living in a blended family.

I have talked to couples who have dated for a very long time, they get married only to discover a very "neat" person has married an all-time "messy" person, whose mess they will now have to live in. I wonder why they never got a clue in all those months of dating. I know why they did not get a clue...they were so in love that they overlooked the red flags. Even if they saw a "messy" red flag, they said to themselves "that will change when we get married." The reality is that if something was there before you married, it will really be there after you are married...and magnified a thousand times. You can have a few messy children in your life, but they will eventually grow up and move out. You can't look forward to a messy spouse leaving home someday. They are already home, and the compromise machine better be oiled and ready for use.

Following close behind the messy chaos issue is the morning person–evening person syndrome. Until you start living up close and personal with someone, it is difficult to tell what the functioning part of their day is. We are all wired differently, and we function well within our own parameters. The conflict comes when daytime and nighttime persons collide. Each feels they have chosen the right way to live and function because that's how they have lived their lives. This is a huge area where compromise has to enter in. Each person has to be willing to move toward a more common ground without having to give up their lifestyle clockwise.

There is a basic question that two people need to ask each other before they choose to marry and create a blended family. If the question is not asked prior to marriage, *it must be asked* when the blended family life begins. The question is, "What can I live with and what can I not live with?" The art of compromise lies within the context of answering that question. We all have break points or deal breakers. We find out what they are when we discover something we choose not to live with.

I have a single male friend who has been divorced for many years. He says he would like to remarry but his deal breaker is he refuses to marry a woman with children. Obviously his field of candidates is limited. If he finds a never-married single woman, she has to give up ever having a child. His field gets narrower, but he is still living with his unwillingness to compromise well into his fifties.

Too many people heading for a second marriage ignore their nonnegotiables until they are married and living in the heart of a blended family. I really believe it is never too late to compromise when both parties are willing, but when one is not, the family will spend a lot of time in the middle of storms. Believing that "love will keep us together" when conflicts are tearing you apart is not facing reality. It is living in a fantasy, and that only works well at Disneyland.

A third area of struggle in a blended family looms when the highly disciplined person marries an undisciplined person. Highly disciplined people spend many years developing their skills. The undisciplined person spends little or no time developing anything and usually allows life to happen where and when it will. Goals and plans take a backseat to living in the moment. This type of blended family union is like teaming a racehorse with a plow horse. They are both horses, and they can look fine until the race starts. After that, it is no contest. Plow horses tend to plow along in life by themselves They need to discover how effective and impactive they could be by learning how to be part of a team. The racehorse person needs to slow down some to allow the plow horse person to run with them.

In these three areas (and yes, there are others), it is not a case of one person being right and one being wrong. It is a case of being different and facing the question, "How can we each make compromises that will help us be a team in our blended family?" We can choose to work through the difficult situations and find compromises in almost all situations.

Looking at Finances and Possessions

In the potential creation of a blended family, I have asked many about to enter that realm a question few people want to answer: "Can you financially afford to climb this mountain?" Very few people think this through before they fall in love with someone. After they are in love, their typical response is, "We can work it out." My questions are "How?" and "What would that look like if you did?" If you do some premarital classes, the facilitators won't let you escape with an easy answer.

It seems rather mercenary to place marriage/blended family formation into the realm of a financial equation, but the truth is it often costs more to create a blended family than to live in a primary family. Outgoing expenses like child support, spousal support, medical plans, and school expenses all add to the blended family picture. Blended families are costly. I don't say that to scare you away or cause you to toss this book in the garbage can. I have already said that I believe in the creation of blended families. I also believe we face our realities in creating them. The financial area is a huge one, and it takes the creative juices of those involved, linked into the active power of God at work in your midst, to deal with it.

Compromise in the financial area of a blended family demands patience, understanding, resourcefulness, and honesty. One of the biggest stress points is often whose children are financially on the inside and whose are on the outside. Many parents tell me they are just waiting for their children to turn 18 so they no longer have to pay child support. I have learned that parents pay for their kids forever! That's a reality.

Possessions are also merged in a blended family unit. Divorce usually leaves a person with one half of everything in possessions. Your half and the half your new spouse got makes a whole, right? No, they usually make a household of badly mismatched furnishings. Sorting out what stays, what goes, and what is valuable to you for any reason is hard work and calls for compromise at its best.

Compromise in Discipline

The big "D"—discipline—goes into the blender in every blended family. Both parents come to the new family with their very own discipline manuals, which they believe are as sacred as the tablets Moses brought down from the mountain. Each manual comes in part from their family of origin, from what they have read in family books, and from the experiences of what has worked for them in the past. When both parents open their manuals of disciplinary instruction, they soon find out there are some things they disagree on. Enter compromise. Take the best from both sides, be united on the standards, make sure all your children understand the game plan and boundaries, and get into gear.

The tough part in establishing good discipline patterns and standards is that you can only work on your side of the fence. What happens in the former spouse's house when your children are there may be vastly different than in your house. Make it clear to all the children that your rules apply in your household. You cannot control what happens in another household. You can scream, protest, and argue about what happens "over there," but you can't really do anything about it. It makes a very unlevel playing field for your children, but fortunately, they are usually bright enough to see what is really happening.

Always be aware that all children can be bribed, and they are childish enough to go with the best deal offered by any parent. The competing parents syndrome usually makes life easier for the children because they win whatever the payoff is. As unfair as this is, my best wisdom over the years is to tell parents to dig in for the long haul. Children grow up and can eventually see the big picture. The things that are unfair will always be there. There are some things you cannot win at. You can only smile, grit your teeth, and move on.

Never Compromise on Love

The blending of "your" children and "my" children when we form a blended family is closely akin to flying a hot air balloon: What we put into it will determine how long it stays up! It takes time and work to get a blended family off the ground and moving in the right direction. Like adults, children come with preformed lifestyles and their very own collection of baggage. Some have been in search of a new parent figure for a long time and will readily accept the stepparent and his or her own children as their brothers and sisters. Others will not, and therein lies the struggle. The two gifts we can give them, mentioned earlier in this book, are still vitally important: time and love. Children have to feel the same sense of security and belonging that adults need to feel. It may take longer because they have not developed adult experiences and reasoning to help them make sense of things. If the new blended family is not good from their perspective, they may hope it will end. If it is good, they may fear it will end like the first family did, and they will lose another family structure they so badly need.

Understanding the needs of the children should have started back when the adults started dating. Adults who have their radar turned on quickly pick up on the family dynamics. If problems were present then and continued to grow, they will become even larger when the new family is formed.

In a first marriage, the parents are both on the scene before the children arrive. In a second marriage/blended family, the children are there before the stepparent arrives. There has been no bonding that slowly took place over months and years. At best, it is a spot welding job, and we sincerely hope and pray the weld holds.

I believe that strong love is not something to be compromised in any way. It is to be offered freely and without expected returns. When planted at the heart of a new blended family, it will take root and grow. Sometimes it feels like we give and nothing comes back in return. The biblical command still says "love one another." It doesn't say you will get good returns from loving. It just says *love*.

FOR DISCUSSION AND PERSONAL RESPONSE

1. In this chapter, what spoke the loudest to you?*

2. How do you plan to implement that in your life?

3. What difference do you feel that will make in your personal life or in the life of your blended family?

4. Who can you call on to help you and hold you accountable to bring that to reailty?

5. List three action steps you will take as a result of reading this chapter.

6. What key role will this chapter play in the long-term growth and development of your blended family?

SEVEN

Key 5:
Acceptance

◼◼◼

IN HIS BOOK *Fully Human, Fully Alive,* John Powell states that there are five things that make a person alive: accepting yourself, being yourself, forgetting yourself in loving, believing in something, and belonging. If you placed those five very human needs alongside Abraham Maslow's "Hierarchy of Needs": psychological, safety, and security, belonging and love, self-esteem and self-actualization, you would have a very accurate picture of the entire span of human needs. We could argue loud and long over which needs should take priority over others. Truthfully, they are all vitally important to our growth and development as members of the human race.

Until we accept ourselves, we cannot fully accept others. If we cannot fully accept others, we run the risk of living in loneliness and isolation. Accepting ourselves is difficult because we are surrounded on all sides by a culture that tells us we must buy a certain product or be different than we are in order to be accepted. Acknowledging yourself and who you are as God's unique, unrepeatable miracle is pushed aside and replaced by the performance push to be acceptable to others. The world of merchandising and advertising sets the bar just beyond human limits to keep us striving for the next rung on the ladder of acceptance. When we are constantly inundated by the secular message that we are not good enough, not acceptable in society, have not climbed high enough on the ladder of success, it is exceedingly difficult to accept ourselves without all the secular attachments.

I believe that self-acceptance has to start by understanding that you and I are God's creative work and that we are loved by God. Remember the first song you learned to sing in Sunday school? For most of us it was "Jesus Loves Me." The first line said, "Jesus loves me! This I know, for the Bible tells me so." There is nothing in this song that talks about first performing for God in order to be loved by him. You and I were created in God's image, and he loves his creative work. If God loves you, can you believe that you can love yourself also?

Many men and women beginning or living in a blended family come in to that experience after being told that someone does not love them any longer. This often translates into believing they are unlovable, and because they are unlovable by others, they cannot love themselves or even remotely believe that God loves them.

People who fight the battle of self-acceptance often waste a lot of energy and effort trying to be someone else only to discover we cannot be something we are not. As little children, we all played the game of pretend. We could become our fictional story or sports heroes and spend hours living in the world of pretend. It usually ended abruptly when we were called to dinner. But finding out who you really are and accepting that person is often a lifetime pursuit. It has to start when you finally realize you have to be authentic and real by accepting yourself with all your warts and weirdness. Authenticity begins when pretend ends. Pretend ends when honesty frees us to say out loud, "This is who I really am!" Any new beginning in our lives is a good time to be real.

Self-acceptability puts us on a personal growth path of self-disclosure. As we grow in self-knowledge, we have a greater ability to be transparent with those around us. We quit worrying about what others may think about us, and we have a new freedom of self-expression.

In many ways, self-acceptance becomes a relational chain reaction. Once we can really accept who we are, we are more accepting of those around us. Why? Because we quit trying to change everyone else so that they will be acceptable to us. When we are free to be who we really are, we set the stage for allowing others to have that same freedom. A self-accepting person creates a climate that sets other people around him or her to be free. Building a healthy blended family begins by setting all the members free to be who they really are and accept their uniqueness as a gift from God. For the children to experience that, it has to be demonstrated by the father and mother.

Key Areas of Acceptance in a Blended Family

Over the years, I have performed many marriages that resulted in the forming of new blended families. The ceremonies vary little from those of first marriages except for the vows and blended family prayer circle we have at the end. Recently, I have wondered what would happen if I included a special segment in the ceremony with both parents and children being involved. In that segment I would share a list of things that need to be accepted in the forming of a blended family. After I read from my list, I would ask each parent if they would accept those things. Then I would present a list to the children and also ask if they would accept the things on that list. After all had said their "I wills," I would offer a benediction and send them off to live an acceptable life and live happily ever after.

If it were that easy, there would be no need for this book. Aside from my wedding list, there are key areas where acceptance needs to be looked at in the life of a blended family. As I said in the beginning of this chapter, letting people be who they are starts on the ground level of self-acceptance. If that is not established first, the important other things on my lists will be difficult to attain.

Accepting Your New Spouse

If the truth were told, in most husband/wife relationships there is a little corner of the mind that said from day one, "There are some things about this person that need to be changed. Given some time, I think I can change them." We all see things in others that we would like to change, and those changes would often benefit the other person. But a good prayer for all of us in this area is by Reinhold Niebuhr. He prayed, "God, grant me the serenity to accept the things I cannot change, the courage to change the things I can, and the wisdom to know the difference."

A new spouse in your newly created blended family comes to you from a previous life where his or her personality has been formed, habits have been honed to perfection, and behavior patterns have been fully developed. Some of these will be hidden and others on full display. Your new mate silently prays that he or she will be loved and understood every day for the rest of his or her life with you. You only catch a tiny glimpse of those things while you are dating the person. They go on full display on the big screen once your new family is formed. The question then asked is, "Can you accept them just as they are or are you ready to send them to redesign school?" Acceptance is an important key to making a marriage work. The acceptance has to be flexible enough to encompass new traits that come along. If it's not, disaster strikes.

She sat in my office huddled in her chair and asked the question several times, "What happened?" She said they had great fun, so much in common, wonderful long talks during the year they dated prior to creating a blended family. They were happy and busy in combined family fun events during that year. Now they had been married almost a year, and the fun was long gone. The family was not living in joyful harmony, money was short, stress was high, and her bubble had burst.

In two years of a relationship, she had gone from "That's Entertainment" to "This Is Reality." Once in the marriage and encircled by their blended family, she discovered the acceptance levels had vanished, and life had become a daily grind. Expectancies died unfulfilled. She felt she could not be herself, and in place of acceptance, she felt rejection.

When I spoke with her husband, he said the woman he accepted and the things he felt she was prior to their marriage had now changed. He asked if I thought she was putting on an act prior to their marriage. The person he had accepted had vanished and he had his own confusion and questions.

Eventually, their marriage ended. The message left with me was, "Be who you are all the time."

What you accept in each other prior to building a blended family should be what you continue to accept with a little variance living in that family. All the history from a former life and family that a spouse brings with them into a new family has to be accepted. They have a history of good and bad that they cannot deny. When a blended family struggle emerges, one of the most painful lines that can be aimed at our spouses is one that reflects on their former marriages or former spouses. When something ties us up in the knots of our past, the pain becomes very real all over again. A spouse's former life experiences are not the bullets to fire when we have already accepted that person into our life. When we accept the person, we accept *everything* about them. Some weapons of war that are used in times of struggle should always be out of bounds. If you get locked in yesterday's war zone, you may need to go back and reread Chapter 4 on forgiveness.

Acceptance of one's spouse in a new family marriage is not "I accept you as you once were" or "I accept you for what you will become," but "I accept you today." Acceptance is renewable every day because the best way to live is by living one day at a time. When we accept another person as he or she is, we leave the responsibility for any changes in God's hands. That is not an easy thing to do because we often feel that God moves too slowly or isn't moving at all. Acceptance of others is a *process* that takes time. Our part of that process is to have a willing spirit and an open heart.

Acceptance creates a safe place where people can grow, feel loved, and belong to others.

Accepting Your Spouse's Children

The key to acceptance in a healthy blended family is often carried in the hands of the children involved. How you respond to them and how they respond to you will dictate the level of harmony in your new family.

When I conducted blended family seminars, I talked frequently about the need to not pit one spouse's children against the other spouse's children. I talked about the fair and even treatment of *all* the children involved and the restraint of any partiality. I also knew that I was wishing on a star in many cases because what I suggested rarely became reality. The truth is, we always tend to favor our own children over the children of others. The "other" children are from a foreign tribe and a foreign country, and the natural human inclination is to keep them at a distance and let your spouse deal with them. But it doesn't have to be this way.

What does accepting your spouse's children look like when lived out? What do you have to do to make that happen? I believe you have to spend time with your new children in order to get to know them and accept them as a part of your world. When you spend time with children, you are telling them they are important to you. When they know they are important to you, it will be easier for them to accept you. In other words, *do* things with them that will enable you to build a friendship with them. This should happen when you are dating someone with children and plan to merge two families. If you did not do it then, you better do it now—and do it often—if your blended family is to work.

Over the years, I have had many children of blended families tell me how much they love and appreciated their stepdad or stepmom. In every case, acceptance and interpersonal involvement over the years won the day.

It's just plain hard to love your spouse's children if they spend all their time getting in your face. And there are many like that that come with some blended family packages. What do you do? Keep loving them and do things that matter to them. Trust that in the long term, things will change for the better. Although some children will never allow you to be a major player in their lives, it should not stop you from fully accepting them into your family. Good seeds planted when they are teens will often bear fruit when they are older and have their own children. Sometimes you need to go the distance with other people's children.

Your spouse's children may live with you full time, part time, or not at all, but that should not change your level of acceptance. The frequent land mines provided by their birth parent/former spouse can be incredibly disruptive to your new blended family. Because children's favorite game is pitting parents against parents so the children can win whatever they are after, it will make your life an obstacle course many days. Going into or living in a blended family, you better decide early on to accept your new mate's children no matter what planet they come from.

From my experience, younger children seem to do better with accepting a stepparent. Teens often appear to struggle hardest with accepting a stepparent. Older children on their own are right up there with teens. They tend to cling to the primary family picture the most and hope to see it restored.

Accepting New Relatives

Some families choose to stay close to each other through a lifetime. Other families have little or no relationship with each other. When primary parents die, their children can drift apart or draw closer to each other. Some family members trade in their family ties for out-of-family support systems. Every family is different and lives out the choices they make, good or bad.

Blended families can be frustrating or fulfilling for their members. The choices for closeness in the family system are often made by those who are not immediate members of the family. When a primary family member chooses to build a blended family, his or her family of origin may draw close or distance themselves from it. Children can divorce and remarry, creating new families that the parents are totally unfamiliar with and may never meet or accept into their family system. Grandparents can get a divorce, remarry, and inherit an entire new family system that never meets other family members.

I have listened to new blended family members tell me they are swamped with new families who want to be a part of their world and others who have told me they are totally isolated from new and even old family members. In a new blended family, we will find ourselves with integration choices. Some will respond in accepting us as a part of their larger family while others will not. We will live out some strange settings that will not change no matter what we do. We can accept people who will not accept us. As I earlier related, my stepfather's family never gave much effort to accepting me no matter what I wanted. It never changed, and I formed no lasting ties with any aunts or uncles. My sister, on the other hand, stayed close to a number of the family members.

What do we do when we are not accepted in a family system? We do the best we can with our part of the acceptance process and keep moving ahead. Some families merge well and others do not. There is little we can do to change that.

In the days prior to blending two families, both spouses should spend time evaluating and looking seriously at what they may face relationally. Most blended family couples I know have just announced their future plans to their families and moved ahead regardless of any negative opinions.

I remember one new blended family father telling me he had inherited all his wife's family, and they were the biggest bunch of nut cases he had ever seen. He did not like any of them even remotely. But he did say that he would honor his wife by accepting them and doing his best to be around them.

It is a huge plus when our new family is truly a "Team Blended Family," and other family members want to be a part of our team. I believe we need all the family members in life that we can collect to make the journey more enjoyable. We can choose those we would like to travel with us, and they can make a similar choice. Life in a blended family doesn't always mean that the relatives will accept us or that we will want to accept them. Where families begin, where they will go, and who will belong to them in their journey through life may largely remain uncharted territories. The best we can often do is simply pray for God's wisdom to guide us as we take the journey.

Accepting My Former Spouse's New Spouse

There is a dimension of blended families that is rarely talked about, thought about, or dealt with. What happens to us when we are happily working to build a blended family and our former spouses announce their marriage plans and their "new" family? How will our family dynamic change? What will we do about accepting our old spouses' new spouses as they impact the lives of the children and our new family?

The most common response I have listened to is, "Great, now he or she will stop bugging me." The second response is, "This is terrible, and it adds one more player and his or her children to an already crowded playing field." The truth is, you will probably face this if you have not already faced it. Another similar variation is your former spouse adds a new player, but they choose to live together and not be married.

One of the biggest wrinkles in a smoothly operating blended family happens when least expected in this area. Your children are quickly placed at the center of this equation because they have to deal with this new person in your former spouse's life. Perhaps even more than you. Typically, they will really like this new person or really hate him or her. And the kids may lean on you to join their team.

Many parents have told me their family picture can change in a blink of an eye, and a whole new complication is tossed into the mix of their blended family. What do we do? We can play denial, but by now we have learned that doesn't work. We can go into a raging tirade against this new player, or we can accept them the best we can.

Blended family members have told me this is bite-the-bullet time. We really can't do one thing about the choice someone else makes. The more energy we use fighting it, the less energy we will have to give to those who need it most. Complaining about our children being around these new players will be less than life-enhancing and accomplishes nothing. That war is never winnable, and all we can do is assume responsibility for the time and input we give our children when they are with us.

Sometimes in this mix is the invitation to the children to come and live with our former spouses and their new mates. This invite most always comes with promises of something the child really wants. A friend of mine calls this a "sneak terrorist attack" on a happy, growing blended family. It comes when we least expect it, and leaves a huge bomb crater.

This, when it happens is not a hill to die on. Stop long enough to build a plan to live with it and accept it. What was that prayer line? "To accept the things you cannot change?" Some wise person said, "The best strategy is to make best friends of your enemy." And I have watched that happen numerous times when a new player runs onto the blended family playing field. Human response is usually negative. When that attitude clears away, accepting the new family member becomes a much more workable way to solve the problem.

How long does it take to accept your former spouse's new player into your mind and family dynamic? It certainly doesn't happen overnight. The amazing thing is, in most cases it all works out and life goes on. It usually takes a huge dose of amazing grace, which God dispenses at just the right time to get us through the conflict.

FOR DISCUSSION AND PERSONAL RESPONSE

1. In this chapter, what spoke the loudest to you?*

2. How do you plan to implement that in your life?

3. What difference do you feel that will make in your personal life or in the life of your blended family?

4. Who can you call on to help you and hold you accountable to bring that to reailty?

5. List three action steps you will take as a result of reading this chapter.

6. What key role will this chapter play in the long-term growth and development of your blended family?

EIGHT

Key 6:
Commitment

MY BRAND-NEW DICTIONARY defines commitment as: "something that takes up time or energy, especially an obligation." The word "commit" is defined as: "to pledge devotion or dedication to somebody or something." What is your definition of these two words? How do they impact your world and the world of your blended family?

We live in a culture today where the words "commit" and "commitment" have taken on a negotiable quality. Athletes sign sports contracts and agree to all the terms but apparently feel they can renegotiate said contracts at any time for any reason. Marriage contracts once formed around the words "till death do us part" could be formed around the words "till problems and disagreements do us part" in today's society. Promises that once had meaning seem to come with exemption clauses today. A person's word, once considered a bond, today means very little. When we are surrounded by a culture that considers nothing as binding, we soon adopt that cultural trait as our own.

I recently asked an about-to-be blended family man how he felt about his upcoming challenge. His response was,

"We'll see how it goes." Surrounded by cultural escape hatches, he already had the exit door in sight. It becomes exceedingly tough to stay the course in a commitment when everyone else is considering their options and exits. Vows and pledges are easier to make than to live out. There are times in wedding ceremonies when vows are concluded that I want to ask the bride and groom, "Did you really mean that?" I am fearful that their answer might be, "Yes, I mean that today. But for tomorrow or next month, we'll see."

In the commitment area, I meet three kinds of people: those who make commitments and keep them, those who make commitments and keep changing or revising them, and those who can't and won't make commitments of any kind, anywhere or at any time. What happens if you are the first kind, and you marry the second or even the third kind? Be prepared for a short trip to the funny farm because committed people are slowly driven crazy by those who want to find ways to get around commitments.

The real struggle most people have with commitments is they do not think through the cost and duration of said commitments. Many men and women are searching for acceptance, and they jump into agreements they are not ready for as a way of gaining that acceptance and the love that goes with it. The best time to assess how people handle commitments is during the dating period. If a person habitually neglects keeping simple commitments, that will only amplify once you are married. If his or her word is not his or her bond while you are dating, it will become bondage in blended family living.

When a second marriage/blended family is established, the primary commitment is always between husband and wife. The deeper their commitment, the greater the chances are to build a healthy blended family. Parents in a blended family—or any family—model what they want their children to learn for their own lives.

I believe the most effective commitments are ones that are personalized and marked in some way to be a reminder of the commitment. My bank knows how to do that well. I signed a contract when I bought my house saying I would make a payment each month for a certain amount. You would think that would be enough to remind me of my commitment to repaying the mortgage loan they gave me. But no, each month they send me a reminder of the amount due and a return payment envelope to send my payment in. They also give me a deadline after which I must pay a late fee. Why is my bank that serious about my commitment? Why are you and I not often that serious about our personal commitments? There is no repossession danger if we don't follow through, no risk of a bad credit rating, no personal embarrassment. My bank and your bank appear to take the commitment we make financially very seriously. Would it be equally important that our personal commitments be treated as seriously as the bank's? I believe that answer is a big *yes!*

What Is the Personal Commitment in a Blended Family Marriage?

Aside from the stated vows and promises made in the marriage ceremony, which I believe are foundational to building a healthy blended family, I believe there are some extremely important commitments that must be added. First, personal commitment means we take ownership of that commitment and in living it out. It does not belong to someone else; it is ours. We can't dismiss it and blame the reasons on another person. It is as much ours as the skin on our body and the air going through our lungs.

The primary commitment is to making this new marriage work. That needs to be stated out loud by both husband and wife to each other and then shared with all the children involved. Obviously, making a marriage work is easier said than done, but it needs to be said before it can be done. This notification also closes the exit doors that offer escape when times get tough. Working on building and growing our blended family will be like training for a marathon run. When we start training, the task before us looks highly improbable except for the fact that others have done what we are about to start doing. After a few months of training, we begin to feel comfortable in our program and begin to really believe we can do this race when race day comes in six months. Building a blended family is like this, except the finish line really only comes when we die. The apostle Paul encouraged the early Christians to "run with patience the race that is set before us" (Hebrews 12:1 KJV). He did not say, "Run like mad, then sit down." Can you say you will run the blended family race, you will be patient and never quit? That's a personal commitment that every man and woman in a blended family needs to think through.

When a marriage license is signed, sealed, and returned for filing with a county clerk, a man and woman indicate together their commitment to marriage. They assume full responsibility to equally share in and build their marriage. They commit individually and collectively to not only make the marriage work, but to make their newly blended family work. The children in that new blended family sign nothing and usually say nothing in the way of making a commitment to helping build their family. The commitment of parents alone in building a blended family is never enough, any more than two players on a sports team being committed to building a winning team can overcome the rest of the players who care little about winning and team building. Children are integral in the future success of the family unit and need to be invited to take ownership in the forming of it.

Remember, a blended family is a team. Team members must all be committed to the building project. The members of a blended family need to commit to bringing out the best in each other. That happens when there is affirmation, encouragement, and love—and they flow in and through the family system. A key question for us to ask is, "What are we committed to as a family?" It may take some time for us to complete our list with everyone's input but it will quickly identify if we are on a growth track and our commitment is unified.

There is a lot of discussion these days about family values. It is talked about, argued about, and discussed to death. Seldom do we hear anyone talk about what those values really look like when a family has them and lives them. A healthy challenge for our blended family would be to spend time in a family forum discussing what those values will be in our family. In a busy world, little if any time is spent talking about what is important in making our family a great family. What is important to the life and health of our family? What things of value do we want to devote time and energy to? What are the standards we choose to live by? What are the things that rob our family of its time and give nothing back in return? (Yes, TV is probably one of them.) What are our family goals, and are they being reached? How is our family different from other families on the planet? Do we give all our energy to the problems that come up and simply exist when there are no problems? What needs to stay in our family life and what needs to go? Are real-life issues discussed, and does everyone have input?

Those are some of the questions that may never be asked if you don't ask them. If you are committed to building a healthy blended family, you will need to wrestle with them.

The Need to Recommit and Renew

I believe all commitments are subject to renewal. Enthusiasm and dedication are the essential ingredients that make any commitment work. The forces of today's culture and the daily race to keep everything going causes the best of us to lose our enthusiasm and dedication. I grew up in a church family that constantly emphasized the fine art of rededicating our lives to God. Our pastor believed that everyday living squeezed the spiritual juices out of us and pushed us off our spiritual track. His emphasis on rededication was to constantly work to get our church family back on track. It seemed we kept on deciding to rededicate so that we could fall away and redo it all over again. Eventually that wore thin. Rather than being told I needed to get back on track, what I really needed were the tools to keep me on track. (Some of those tools we will talk about in the next chapter.) But there is a place for renewing commitments that we have made. When we do that, no matter how or where, we are still saying our commitment is strong and unchanging. We need that reminder to get us back on our spiritual tracks or to simply keep us on them. Life without reminders is a life with no memory of commitments made and renewed.

Many churches have marriage renewal ceremonies each year. Those who want to renew their vows can do so. It would be healthy for churches to have blended family renewal times when entire family units can stand before the church family and reaffirm the commitments they want to maintain.

One of the most powerful commitments made in the Old Testament was made by Joshua. In the last days of his life, Joshua was challenging Israel to serve and follow God. As he asked for their commitment, he put his own on the line when he said: "But as for me and my household, we will serve the LORD" (Joshua 24:15). When such strong commitments are made, someone has to lead in making them. I believe that in a blended family, the mantle of leadership rests upon the father. The sharing in fulfilling those commitments rests upon every member of the family unit.

When a blended family is established, a man and a woman make a marriage commitment to each other. They also make a commitment to building a blended family together. That commitment grows in ever-widening circles when the children in that family become committed to each other, committed to their parents, and committed to building their blended family.

When commitments are strong, blended families are healthy!

FOR DISCUSSION AND PERSONAL RESPONSE

1. In this chapter, what spoke the loudest to you?*

2. How do you plan to implement that in your life?

3. What difference do you feel that will make in your personal life or in the life of your blended family?

4. Who can you call on to help you and hold you accountable to bring that to reailty?

5. List three action steps you will take as a result of reading this chapter.

6. What key role will this chapter play in the long-term growth and development of your blended family?

NINE

Key 7:
Being Spiritually Centered

A LOT OF THOUGHT AND PLANNING goes into the house a blended family chooses to live in. Size, location, affordability, design, and decor are all well thought through in a house search. The comfort of each family member is also high on the list. Once those issues are settled, the new family can move in and go about the business of living their lives. Schedules, wardrobes, food, chores, work, homework, and sports become daily and weekly issues to be taken care of. These are everyday things in most families' lives and seldom vary until the children are grown and gone. We give energy, thought, and a lot of planning in those areas, but we often give minimal thought to one important component—making a family spiritually centered.

Some readers will say they are spiritually centered because they go to church, have a few Bibles lying around, pray at mealtimes, and believe in God. I am glad if you do those things but does that make you and your family spiritually centered? I grew up in a good church youth group that pretty much dictated the Christian lifestyle of its members. We had a long list of things we were not supposed to do because we were Christians. We had a second list of the things we were supposed to do because we were Christians. Most of us in the group fell somewhere in between the two lists from time to time. We all claimed a sense of spirituality because of what we did and did not do. It took me many years on my spiritual journey to discover that I needed to move from being a Christian "doing" to being a Christian actively living my faith. That performance part still lingers at the edge of my life. It is often easier to "do" something than to "actively live" something.

To live out my Christian faith may mean that I have certain attitudes I need to change. Perhaps I may need to get involved in charitable acts that will help others. Or maybe I must be willing to be inconvenienced from time to time without getting angry. Actively living my Christianity may mean loving people who are not easy to love and doing things that aren't fun. These things are defined as actions and attitudes that demand something from me. Through Christ I can do these things...and He will bring about change in me. I can go to church and something that may happen there may bring about a needed change in my life, but the physical act of "doing church" in and of itself does not demand much from me. Many people who attend church can be compared to people who attend sporting events. They sit, watch, applaud, make a little noise, and go home or out to lunch. It really doesn't demand much interpersonal involvement or brain power. They just watch and observe.

When Jesus called the disciples to a life of change, he said, "Follow me...and I will make you fishers of men." He never said, "Follow me and I will make you observers of men." The disciples were called to a life of active involvement; they were called to be something they had little or no experience in. But they were called to a lifestyle that was comparable to what they knew, which was fishing. Only their targets were people, not fish. Their new life gave them a new spiritual center—Jesus.

When we establish a new blended family, it is vital to have a spiritual center for ourselves and our families. In most families, blended or otherwise, little time or energy is ever devoted to open discussion and evaluation of spiritual things. There are "religious" things to attend and "religious" things to observe. I call them religious because I am not always sure they fall into the category of "Christian." I meet many people who go to every function their church has to offer, yet they never explore what it means to be spiritually centered.

If you are trying to build a Christian blended family, I challenge you to personally work on my questions and invite your family to explore them with you. What does a spiritually centered blended family look like? And how would that family be different than a nonspiritually centered family? I believe you will be totally amazed at what you will hear and learn. Let me share some things that others have found by accepting my challenge.

The first really big thing is a directive that Jesus gave his disciples: Love one another (John 13:34). At the very core of a spiritually centered family, *agape* love should dictate how that family operates. The Greek word *agape* means "unconquerable benevolence. Love with no limitations." Hard to do, difficult to envision, but totally necessary. None of us are lovable 24/7. Loving each other happens when we commit to that as a lifetime goal and make that the core of our belief system spiritually. God's love for you and me echoes loudly from John 3:16: "For God so loved the world that he gave his one and only Son, that whoever believes in him shall not perish but have eternal life." That verse was the starting point for most of us when we decided to follow Jesus. That decision put us into living the Christian life. We then accepted the responsibility to live our lives from a spiritual center. What happens is we often lose sight of that center and replace it with things that sound and look good but don't offer what we really need.

One of the great ways we experience God's love firsthand is through people loving us. What better place to experience that love than at the center of our families! There are always ways to demonstrate love, but it also needs to be verbalized. "I love you" are words that when vocalized can be life-changing. When spoken, the challenge is to receive the demonstration of the words.

A number of years ago, I worked on the church staff of a church known today as The Crystal Cathedral. In every service, the senior pastor, Dr. Robert Schuller, would have the congregation stand, turn, and shake hands with the people around them and say, "God loves you, and I love you!" I was always glad that I was on the platform rather than in the pew. I wondered what would happen if I told someone "God loves you, and I love you." Would they say, "Thank you, but do you love me enough to come over next Saturday and help me paint my house?" When we tell people we love them, they may transform the words and thoughts into a tangible request that requires an action response from us. Love then becomes something we do not just say.

At the heart of a spiritually centered blended family, love is taught as an action word. Family members should be encouraged to say "I love you" to any other family member at any time. A good test to see if they're responding to this love is to listen to your family for a week and count the number of times the words "I love you!" are said from one family member to another. Setting your family free to say that is a personal challenge for you. And don't forget to make that affirmation frequently yourself. I believe a spiritually centered family that is anchored to God needs to create an atmosphere where love is spoken and acted upon. Jesus did not say "I suggest you love one another" to the disciples. He said "A new command I give you: Love one another." God's love and our love for each other must be at the core of every spiritually centered blended family.

Bill Taegel, in his book *People Lovers*, tells us there are three kinds of love: "If love," "Because love," and "Anyhow love." He says the first two are based upon conditions we place on other people. We love them *if* they love us first, *if* they are kind and good to us and do certain things for us. In other words, they first have to perform for us in order to receive our love. Some parents love their children in this way. As long as the children do the right things, they will be rewarded with their parents' love. If you operate like that, *stop!* It is an unhealthy way to teach anyone about love.

Because love is similar to *if* love. It is love after the fact. Someone has already done the things to earn our love, and now we can dispense that love. It is still performance and deed based. Sadly, the first two kinds of love are widespread in our culture and family life. It becomes a system of rewards for behavior lived out.

Anyhow love simply says I will love you no matter what. It is *agape* love. Jesus taught this kind of love. It is love with no limitations and obstacles. It means we know how to separate good or bad performance from the act of loving someone. We are always free to tell our children we totally disagree with something they have done and believe it is wrong for them, but we still love them. Most of us can get entangled in the deed, and allow that deed to withhold our love from a person.

Is agape love too tough to embrace and too demanding to live out? If you believe what Jesus said about love, you better get into training because there is no option clause here. We are commanded to love. There is no more fertile soil in which to plant the seeds of love than in your blended family. One of the true tests of love is loving someone else's children as much as your own.

In the Country-and-Western music field, the songs tell about love lost or love betrayed. In the contemporary field, love songs tell about expressing love from one person to another and the benefits of love from one person to another. One old song starts out with, "What the world needs now is love, sweet love, it's the only thing that there's just too little of." If the world needs love, you need it at the center of your blended family.

Spiritually Centered Transitions

He said, "It's going to be different this time." We had been talking about building a spiritually centered home for the past hour. The wedding day was fast approaching, and a new blended family would soon be born. Lou did not want his new family to look like his past family. He told me his former marriage wasn't a pagan environment. It had religious trappings, religious holiday observances, and an old family Bible prominently displayed. But it was not spiritually centered. His own search for a deeper faith in God began shortly after his devastating divorce. As his spiritual journey began to deepen, Lou made a personal decision to place God at the center of his family if he ever remarried.

Sometimes God uses a wake-up call to get us on the right track. Countless men and women who have gone through the loss of a marriage have expressed their determination to put God first in the rest of their lives. They chose to spiritually center their lives and vowed to do the same for any new family they might someday be a part of. Many expressed that God was on the fringes of their first family's attention but never got to center stage. Some even said they grew up in spiritually centered families but married someone with no interest in that.

I define spiritually centered transitions as collecting all you know about God from your life experiences to date and being willing to explore new ground spiritually for yourself and any new family situation you are living in. These questions may help you explore that opportunity.

1. How would you define where you are spiritually right now?

2. What spiritual experiences have you had that you can draw from?

3. Do you feel you are spiritually centered right now?

4. What does being spiritually centered look like to you?

5. What is your biggest spiritual need right now?

6. What are the steps to fulfilling that need?

7. What is the first thing you need to do?

8. What resources are available to you?

9. What three goals would you set for yourself spiritually right now?

These nine questions demand some head and heart time on your part. This is not a quiz to answer right or wrong to. They are the beginning steps of a plan to center your life spiritually. The questions are personal, but they can also be asked in a family setting as family members give their input for forming a family plan.

The transition from what we know and have experienced spiritually to exploring a new, deeper relationship with Christ can be difficult because we tend to fall back on what we know and what makes us feel comfortable. Jesus was not about creating a comfort zone for his followers. He trained them daily to get out on the playing field in life and take risks. We risk upheaval when we work on the hard questions. But upheaval can be a refreshing, revitalizing opportunity!

Spiritually Centered Components for Your Blended Family

There are a number of different things you can add to your blended family to keep the center strong spiritually. Some you may already have, some you may not. And there are some tools you can bring into your home that will help create a spiritual environment.

What your children watch on TV can powerfully influence their lives. Why not offset some of that secularism with Christian materials? Christian bookstores have a wide array of Christian videos and DVDs from which you can build your own library. Coupled closely to that are Christian CDs. I am amazed at the wide variety of music available today in the Christian marketplace. What sounds do you want coming out of your home? What messages do you want your children to hear? What do you want them to read? Christian literature has an exhaustive selection of good reading for all ages today. The messages children need to hear to give them a spiritual foundation are readily available. They won't know what to buy, but you will. Christian bookstores are packed to the rafters with incredibly helpful tools for your entire family.

About every home on planet Earth is decorated in some way, shape, or form. In our recent search to buy a home, I found myself asking "What kind of people live here?" as I looked at books on shelves, CDs, wall hangings, and so forth. What is in our homes and how they are decorated says something very strong about what we believe. Christian symbols and artwork can make a statement of faith to all who visit and also remind those who live there what they believe and why they believe it. I am not suggesting that your home become a religious art gallery. But it could contain visible signs that mean something to you about your spiritual walk. A friend of mine had an artist paint the words "As for me and my house, we will serve the Lord," on one of her walls. It is there for Christian and non-Christian friends to see and think about. It is her faith statement for her family, even though some of the members are not sharing her faith journey at this time.

One of the most visible signs of a spiritually centered family I have seen over the years is a room designated as a prayer room. It is usually a small, out-of-the-way place with a place to kneel and pray, a chair to sit and read in, and a Christian symbol of meaning on one wall. Some even have a candle on a stand to light. It is a welcoming and quiet spiritual environment that calls family members to come and be silent and prayerful before the Lord. Busy airports and hospitals have prayer chapels...why not your home? On a speaking trip several years ago, I was in a home that had a prayer garden in the backyard. As I looked at it, it seemed to say, "Come and sit with the Lord here."

These are only a few of the components you can use in your home to encourage the building of a spiritually centered family.

Being Spiritually Centered Out There

Having a spiritually centered home is vital to our survival spiritually, but it is equally important that we take what we have in our homes into the world around us. One of the ways I have watched blended families do that is by becoming involved in community outreach projects. Some of these are church-sponsored, and you can just join in. Others are based in the community, and you can volunteer some time each week and take family members with you. Cooking at the mission, feeding the poor and homeless, and working at halfway houses are a few of the hundreds of activities usually available in every community.

Another opportunity is taking your family on a mission trip for a few days or several weeks in a foreign country. One church I know of sends 25 mission teams every year to foreign countries. These teams include entire families, single adults, retired folks, young and old alike. The incredible stories and softened hearts that return from those trips remain for lifetimes. Travel and exposure to other cultures and socio-economic areas are important. Children today need to see the impact of poverty and sickness so they won't become insensitive to the world they live in. Our world is no longer obscurely compartmentalized. Television alone drops everything onto your family room floor. We can see the world with little personal impact or become actively involved in making it a better place.

Jesus' command to go into all the world did not end when the disciples died. Families today have a window on the world that is large and ever-expanding. Spiritually centered families know the inward and outward call.

Finding a Church Home

A divorce often causes you to leave your old church home and find a new one. Single-again people need a church with an effective singles ministry where they can find community. Not all churches offer that, nor do they always welcome divorced men and women. Churches that do not welcome hurting people who have come looking for hope and healing aren't fulfilling their job. How does your church support you? Will your church be the best place for your new family to attend? Use the following questions to evaluate your current situation.

1. How does your church help you become a more spiritually centered family?
2. What does your church do to equip you and your family to be healthier?
3. Is there a blended family support group in your church?
4. Are you able to serve as a leader in your church even though you're divorced?
5. Is your church a healing church or a condemning church?
6. Are the needs for your children to grow spiritually being met?
7. Why do you attend your church?
8. Are you in your church by default or divine direction?

9. Do you know the pastoral staff, and do they know you?

10. Have you and your family officially joined your church?

If you look for a new church home, call the churches for basic information. Have them send you everything they have in print about themselves. When you visit with your blended family, do a debriefing later in the day and collect everyone's input. If it is generally good, decide to give the church a two-month trial visitation. You need to see it at different times with different people involved. Every church has an off-Sunday periodically. You don't want to judge the church on one Sunday alone.

If the church is looking like a place you can call home, make appointments with the senior pastor and other staff pastors to get to know them. You will feel better in the audience of worship if you feel the people on the platform are your friends rather than strangers.

If the church is large, find a few smaller places where you can connect. It isn't important to know everyone, but it is crucial to know a few someones. If there is a blended family support group, join it. If there isn't, see if you can start one. Resist just becoming a spectator at the worship services and then going home. Being a visitor every Sunday does not give you a home. Taking ownership in a church will make you feel at home and will give you a growing sense of belonging. Get involved!

You! The Spiritually Centered Person

When we made the decision to follow Jesus and turn our lives over to him, we faced the challenge to draw closer to the Lord. Second Peter 3:18 says we are to "grow in the grace and knowledge of our Lord and Savior Jesus Christ." There is no finalization of growth in this life. Only when we stop breathing, do we stop becoming spiritually strong. Until then we are all on a spiritual journey, and we are to work at becoming spiritually centered. There is no place to drop off the growth curve in our Christian lives. To read, study, pray, and move forward is the challenge. If there is a goal in that, I believe it is spiritual maturity. We cannot lead our families spiritually unless we are on the road to spiritual growth.

A good measurement stick in spiritual maturity is to answer the question, "Am I further ahead in my spiritual growth now than I was a year ago? Three years ago? Five years ago?" If the answer is no, no, and no, I suggest you purchase a copy of the book *Experiencing God* by Henry Blackaby and Claude King. Get inside the pages and let God speak to your life so that your life can speak to others. Then find a trusted Christian who can mentor you for a while and help you move ahead.

Very few people ask you how you are doing spiritually. Somehow, no matter how many Bible classes you take or prayer meetings you attend or don't attend, no one will pop up and hit you with the big question: "How are you doing spiritually?" So, if no one does, ask yourself and answer honestly. If you are heading up a blended family, you need to be spiritually fit to the task.

1. In this chapter, what spoke the loudest to you?*

2. How do you plan to implement that in your life?

3. What difference do you feel that will make in your personal life or in the life of your blended family?

4. Who can you call on to help you and hold you accountable to bring that to reailty?

5. List three action steps you will take as a result of reading this chapter.

6. What key role will this chapter play in the long-term growth and development of your blended family?

10

Living the Seasons
in a Blended Family

MOST OF OUR JOURNEY THROUGH LIFE is marked by stages. We may not like the ones we have to pass through to get to better places, but we rarely can avoid the struggles if we want to really grow, change, and become healthier.

In divorce recovery, we talk about shock, recovery, and growth. These three stages are universal to any painful or traumatic situation a human being may face. Beyond the panic and pain, there is always the rebuilding and new growth. The difficult part for us to understand is that these processes take time to navigate. Being creatures of an instant culture, anything that takes time leaves us looking for shortcuts that will get us to our destination more rapidly.

There are real growth stages in the overall process of blending your life and family with the life and family of another person. I believe there are some real similarities between the four seasons of the year—spring, summer, fall, and winter—and the seasons that blended families go through on their road to maturity. By examining these we can gain fresh new insights into our new life in a blended family.

In nature, *spring* typifies new life, new beginnings, and a fresh start. It signifies the closing of a dull, drab, slushy, cold season. Spring is planting time and awakening time. The windows of hope are wide open to newness. Spring in a blended family is when all the planting, nurturing, and preparation for the years ahead is born. It is when the risks are taken and the trust assured. The soil of life is stirred with the confidence of a gardener who has done his or her homework. Questions and uncertainties about new relationships may take root. Fears can still linger around the edges of this new blended family and are only put to rest as authentic relationships are given the chance to grow.

Spring in a blended family is when questions are asked, inner fears confessed, mistakes owned, and plans and dreams for the future are shared. It is a time to grow slowly, and it cannot be hurried. Like plants we put into the ground, great care must be exercised to ensure future growth.

The spring in a blended family is a time to enjoy. A sense of romance that was long lost or never experienced in a former marriage takes root. Spring brings a sense of vitality and adventure. New people are now a growing part of our lives. We are creating a new beginning together.

This special season is a preparation time for planting the right things in the lives of those involved to encourage the family's success. The seven keys to a healthy blended family mentioned in this book are the fertilizer that guarantees good growth. If we want to eventually smell the flowers, we must first be willing to smell the fertilizer.

How long does spring last in a blended family? Until all the groundwork is done and the root systems are in place. There are no quantum leaps from one season to another in nature, and there are no bypasses from one season to another in blended families.

Summer! It never comes soon enough when we are children. There's no more school and endless days of doing just what we want. Schedules are relaxed or nonexistent. All of that is true when we are under 16 years of age. Beyond that, we work and go to summer school and get ready for fall and more school. For parents, about the only change is we get to experience summer vacation but work fulltime before and after that interlude. Still, most of us would wish for an endless summer if we could.

What does the season of summer look like in a blended family? It is still a time of adjustment for everyone, but the permanence of this new experience is more accepted. There is more excitement about belonging to this new place and trusting one another to enjoy the journey. One blended family mother expressed her feelings recently by simply saying, "At long last, I feel the pressure is off." Notice, she did not say "over." She said they had planted the right seeds in the right places in the spring of their blended family and now those seeds had grown, making life more relaxed and enjoyable.

Having fun is a vital part of the summer season. Going to new places, doing new things, and celebrating life together is at the heart of that fun. Summer means more time to talk and build deeper relationships. It is also a time when children may go to be with their primary parent for weeks at a time, leaving a gaping hole in their new blended family. As some children leave, other children who live with the other parent may appear for weeks at a time. A designated summer of fun can quickly turn into a summer of conflict and unrest for those who would rather be any place than where they are. Adjusting to the inclusion of those from other places is seldom easy and takes a great deal of grace to navigate. But summer is still a time to celebrate.

The words of one blended family father will always echo in my mind. He said, "The happiest day of the year is when my children come to spend the summer with us. The saddest day is when they return home to the other parent." From my experience, about half of all blended families split the time the children spend with each family in the summer. For a stepparent, this can be a fearful time because incoming children are often an unknown quantity in lifestyles, behavior, and personality. It can also be a time of building a healthy and growing relationship with them. Relationships built during the summer can be maintained long distance during the other seasons.

Family continuity that may have existed in your former marriage may become a different commodity in a blended family. The more people involved in the decision-making process, the more complicated the script. That summer of fun may be harder to obtain, but it still is worthwhile to pursue and enjoy.

The season of *fall* is usually harvest time. In nature, it is the result of planting, watering, growing, and coming of age. In a blended family, it symbolizes a maturity that is the result of a good spring and summer of daily work and growth. That maturity settling-in lets us know that we did not marry into a perfect situation, but the imperfect is workable and will not defeat us. In the life of a blended family, the fall season often occurs somewhere between two to five years.

Looking at blended families over the past 28 years, I have watched two predominant things happen in this fall season. The first is watching a blended family grow strong and healthy, leave the past in the past, and march toward the future with a solid game plan and creative family goals.

Relationships are strong and secure, and the family has planted deep roots for all involved. That's the good news.

The second thing that happens in the fall season is that often the fabric of the family is stretched thin, the relationships weaken, the members take each other for granted, and the odds of disintegration grow and place the family on the edge of a second divorce. Trust in the concept of a blended family disappears, and hope for its members dies. The good new is that there are several things that can move us away from the collapsing edge.

1. Let reality take over from fantasy. Fantasy says we can live forever with our heads in the clouds and our feet firmly planted in thin air. Reality says we have to do the homework, pay the bills, discipline the children, take care of the house, fix the car, and so forth. There are no perfect people living in blended families.

2. Realize there are as many myths in blended families as there are in primary families. Trade in any myths we might have for large doses of reality. Understand and know that stable people cannot anchor their lives to myths.

3. Watch out for the ruts. The same things that sidetracked a first marriage can cause problems in a second marriage. The reason many people repeat patterns is that they are familiar and comfortable with them.

4. Do frequent blended family reviews. Ask the hard questions. Go over and work on the problem areas. Update our plans and goals. Get input from everyone involved in the new family structure.

5. Stop looking for exits and start looking for entrances. Don't take the easy way out if the family isn't what was expected. Go to work, and make it what it should be.

The fall is time for bringing blended families to solid maturity. This season may call upon everything we possess as we in turn call upon God for his strength.

In nature, *winter* means a time of rest before the coming of spring. In a blended family season, it means that time after five years when the family and its members know that the foundation is solid, and the family can rest upon that foundation and never be dislodged. Realities have been accepted, solutions to problems have been found, adjustments have been made, and love has grown in all the members. It is at this juncture that we have to remind the members of the blended family that they are a blended family. Members often feel like their lives have always been lived in this structure. The "before" has faded and the "now" has taken its place. Thoughts of primary family will always be there, and should be there. But the blended family model has grown so strong that former memories are filed away.

As a pastor, I often talk with couples I have united over 10 to 20 years ago. They seldom, if ever think of themselves as remarried or part of a blended family. I have watched them grow as individuals and couples. I have watched their children and stepchildren grow and build their own lives. I have witnessed the love and admiration they have for one another as extended family members. They and their families have made the journey from spring through winter. They have refused to become additional statistics and fatalities in the land of blended families. They are the continuing reasons I believe in remarriage and the creation of blended families.

For Discussion and Personal Response

1. In this chapter, what spoke the loudest to you?*

2. How do you plan to implement that in your life?

3. What difference do you feel that will make in your personal life or in the life of your blended family?

4. Who can you call on to help you and hold you accountable to bring that to reailty?

5. List three action steps you will take as a result of reading this chapter.

6. What key role will this chapter play in the long-term growth and development of your blended family?

ELEVEN

Adding Branches to the Family Tree

RESEARCHING AND CONSTRUCTING your family tree is an exhausting but fulfilling experience. In the first 40 years of your life, that kind of challenge seems dull and uninteresting. We already have too much to do and too little time to do it. As we inch toward that 50-something decade, something inside us wants to trace roots and ancestries. If it hasn't been done, we begin the quest that is prompted by the question, "Where did I come from?"

Buried in one of my files is a folder depicting the long and storied history of my family on my primary father's side. Fortunately a family member did all the work, and I can look through the branches of my tree as far back as the early 1800s. I don't spend much time pulling out that folder anymore, but I will pass the information on to my children.

When a divorce or death of a spouse happens, families often drift away from their root systems. When a new blended family is formed, branches are grafted onto our family tree that will forever change its original form. If I were to draw an average schematic of the ways that a family tree can change and become increasingly complex, we would have a hard time keeping track of all the new branches.

Leading the parade of new branches are a group called grandparents. When a new blended family is formed, grandparents often find themselves cut off from the family tree in some way or dangling out on the end of its branches wondering how they got there. Grandparent structures are often split, splintered, and lost when a divorce hits a family. When a remarriage follows, they can end up even further removed from the viable and caring relationships they once had with their children and grandchildren. Grandchildren can be shuffled out of state when a new blended family is formed, and relationships that were once significant deteriorate and die.

When a blended family is formed, new sets of grandparents with former family connections to the primary unit come riding over the hill to meet the new challenges. They often want to forcefully assume their new role, much to the chagrin of the new children. Sometimes the children welcome the new grandparents, only to face rejection by them. At other times, the children reject the grandparents and a relational rift is formed in the family system.

Acceptance or rejection are the two most common experiences by both children and adults when grandparents are added to the family tree. When one's former spouse also remarries, another grandparent system is grafted onto the family tree. The thought of having an annual blended family reunion with the incredible variations relationally is mentally staggering.

I personally believe that parents need all the help they can get in raising their children. I believe that grandparents are a vital part of that child-raising process. My grandparents on my mother's side of the family filled an incredible place in my life growing up. The farther I felt distanced from my stepfather's family, the closer I got to my maternal grandparents. What did they offer me? Love, acceptance, and support. They were there for me!

How do you navigate the grandparent rapids in a blended family? When grandparents are grafted on as new branches, your children are also grafted onto their family tree. Both are responsible to make the new connection work. Here are a few suggestions from the vantage point of my experience.

1. If you are a new stepgrandparent, don't expect an overnight miracle of acceptance by new stepgrandchildren. Spend time getting to know them by being with them. Find out about their lives, interests, histories, dreams, and goals. Don't investigate them and don't ask questions that are personal intrusions into their past life. Be wise and kind.

2. Invite new stepgrandchildren into your life. They need to know all about you as well. Think permanent connection with them. You want to build lifelong friendships.

3. If you are a stepparent, make sure you create opportunities for your own children and stepchildren to spend time with the new stepgrandparents. If you are the parent, explain the kind of relationship you would like your parents to have with your children and vice versa. Don't ignore grandparents if they live in another state.

4. Create situations for family gatherings where all the in-step and non-instep members can be together.

Even if the situation feels nontraditional to you, and it will, it is your new reality. Developing a feeling of comfort with the new branches of your family tree will be work, and it will take time. Don't give up because your new family doesn't gel quickly.

5. Create an open and welcoming spirit for any and all entering your new family tree. Grandparents add a dimension to the lives of all children that no other relatives can. Active grandparents need to be accessible and involved with *all* their grandchildren.

6. Don't waste time chasing people who don't want to be a part of your family tree. Some grandparents are simply not blendable. Your own parents may not be wonderful grandparents to your children and that can hurt.

The Other Branches

After the grandparents, there is usually an endless column of aunts, uncles, nephews, nieces, assorted cousins, and former in-laws. Where do they fit on your new family tree? What if they don't?

Looking over all the possibilities of a new family structure would be akin to looking over the crowd at a sporting event and wondering how we could invite some of them to become friends with us. If we did, we would have to invest two things: time and initiative.

I believe the same is true for potential relatives. We have to invest something to receive something back. If we reach out, some will reach back and others will not. Some will form a supportive community around us and embrace us, while others will not give us the time of day. Remember, they were there before we arrived. We are the new people. Instant acceptance and inclusion rarely happen. Those new about-to-be-grafted branches also have feelings about how we got into their family system. They may still like the people we replaced and will not want to show loyalty to us.

There are a ton of feelings and emotions that come with those new branches of our family tree. Sometimes they need to be worked through before they can have a meaningful relationship with us and our children. We will seldom envelop a new blended family into a preexisting family without some bumps in the road. Blend where we can and add those to our new family who are supportive, loving, and caring. Often the numbers may be small but the quality can be high.

Loose Ends on the Family Tree

There will always be some loose ends in a blended family structure. If you are the kind of person who doesn't live well with loose ends, this will be difficult for you. One of the never-ending loose ends is finding the precarious balance between you, your children, your current spouse, and your former spouse. One of my friends describes a former spouse as a leaf that fell off the family tree but never gets raked and burned. A former spouse will always be a former spouse. That status will never change. They will also forever be the birthparent of your children. That will never change. Birthdays, holidays, vacations, and special times seldom fall into a livable and always-agreeable pattern for all the members of a blended family. The eternal battle is usually over "who gets whom for how long on what days." Children become the spoils of a constant tug of war. This often causes a child to end up bitter and angry later in life and not relate well to either parent. To make the transitions smoother and more congenial, I work long and hard with former spouses to help them become friends rather than enemies in the new blended family systems. If there is a constant conflict, the wearing effect can grind us down emotionally and disrupt our new families.

It is equally important that a new spouse not get caught in conflict with their new spouse's former spouse. Sound confusing? It is, and feelings can run very high on a daily basis concerning issues such as discipline, fairness, obligations, and finances. Remember, it is not your job to tie up someone else's loose ends.

When we enter a second marriage that comes with children attached, we don't just marry that little group. We actually marry an entire family system that may be highly functional and enjoyable to be a part of or we could inherit a very dysfunctional family system that has had years of practice at being dysfunctional. It is always good to check that out before we say "I do." And, if our blended families are already up and running, we need to carefully pick our way through the minefields and decide what branches we want to permanently attach to our tree.

FOR DISCUSSION AND PERSONAL RESPONSE

1. In this chapter, what spoke the loudest to you?*

2. How do you plan to implement that in your life?

3. What difference do you feel that will make in your personal life or in the life of your blended family?

4. Who can you call on to help you and hold you accountable to bring that to reailty?

5. List three action steps you will take as a result of reading this chapter.

6. What key role will this chapter play in the long-term growth and development of your blended family?

TWELVE

Blended Families
Speak Out

THE LEARNING PROCESS for most of us entails observation and implementation. Perfecting what we learn comes through a trial-and-error process. I doubt there is a blended family anywhere that has gone from inception at the altar of marriage to flawless perfection in the first week of blended family living. We can read all the guide books for blended family living in print and find them helpful and practical. But until we actually become a player on a blended family team and get in the game, all the good principles on earth will have little impact on us. I believe most of us need less "how to" and more "you're doing great at this" support. Instruction without affirmation seldom warms our hearts and helps us keep going.

I recently asked a veteran group of blended family people to share what words of wisdom from their own journey they would want others to know. Their voices of experience are written in italics, with my comments following theirs.

1. *Before committing to the marriage, look for pitfalls, problems, trends, and quirks during dating that could become issues*

after marriage. Don't let your expectations cloud the reality of the relationship. How do you do that when you are blinded by love? You have one or two accountability friends ask you the hard questions and keep you focused—and you listen to what they have to say. It is easier to work on potential snags and potholes *before* the marriage than after. After you marry, you may need the wise guidance of a qualified counselor or pastor to work through difficult issues.

2. *Find solutions early to avoid conflict later.* One of the best ways to do that is to ask questions. When you see a potential problem or difference on anything, instead of criticizing or judging, ask, "How can we work at solving that difference?" Most people resent being "told" but welcome being "asked." Questions initiate discussion, and problems are solved through shared discussion. Remember, what isn't solved *before* you remarry will be more difficult to solve after your blended family is created.

3. *Don't bury conflict—face it head on.* When conflict arises, most of us do one of two things: We fight or take flight. Neither is highly constructive in conflict resolution. Earlier in this book, I shared that communication is a key to a healthy family. Communication is talking *and* listening, with the emphasis on listening. Listening and asking the right questions lets you really see inside the conflict and work toward resolution. What you detect in a person prior to remarriage is what you will live with after remarriage.

4. *Break down walls.* We build walls in our lives for two reasons: isolation and protection. Walls keep us from venturing out and running the risk of being hurt. Walls keep others away from us, and keeps the hurt they may inflict

away. We all have a few walls in our lives that we need to turn into bridges. Bridges help us over and through the fearful places that have caused us to erect the barriers. Someone said, "People are lonely because they build walls instead of bridges." Walls that are present prior to building a blended family will only get thicker and higher after that family is created. A great discussion question is, "Where are the walls in your life and why are they there?"

5. *Premarital counseling/testing is a must. Post-marital counseling for the first year in your blended family is also necessary, whether you think you need it or not.* Many of you are already living in a blended family that had no counseling before it was established. Is it too late now? No. In fact, counseling is very important now. Everyone needs navigational help from time to time. That can come from trusted counselors, pastors, and friends. One of my pet peeves is that many churches offer premarital classes for those contemplating marriage. When the class is complete, the marriage takes place, the honeymoon happens, and life begins…and no one ever again asks if we are doing okay or if we need any help. There is no one-year, five-year, ten-year checkup. For all intents, we are abandoned to our own way of existence, and everyone assumes we will be fine. But those who should care about our progress don't offer much if anything in the way of guidance for our journey. My advice is simple: Get what you need when you need it. The following suggestion is right on target.

6. *Use seminars and support groups to learn, give you vision, and put things in perspective.* Look for them or ask your church to help you start them. Connect to other blended families.

7. *The first year will be the toughest but things get better with time.* The one big sign I would hang over the first year for every blended family is *adjustment.* Throughout this book, I have talked about the many adjustments you will face. You will feel that you are running through an obstacle course for a year or longer. The challenges are like the pop-ups on your computer. They just keep coming from some hidden recess in the caves of technology.

You will need a few good people in your life during that year that you can share with. Most blended family members want to know that what they are facing is normal, it will pass, and they will survive.

8. *Commitment is the key.* Go back and read the chapter on commitment, then say to yourself, "When faced with a mountain, I will not quit!" Ask God to give you daily strength for your journey and to help you keep moving forward.

9. *Love each other, put your spouse's feelings first, and don't be selfish.* That's a life-building project you work on one day at a time. It will never be easy because you may have been raised with the "look out for yourself first and put everyone else in second place" mentality. It's work to turn that around, and you may need someone to be accountable to for help.

10. *Give each other the right to be right.* We are all wrong… some of the time, and we are all right…some of the time. And no one should be keeping score. If this is a struggle for you, try saying the words "you are right" out loud 20 times a day to get used to the idea of saying it. We all want desperately to be right. It makes us feel good when we are,

but we also have to learn to say "I was wrong" when we know we were wrong. That's the right thing to do.

11. *Know your boundaries.* Everyone needs boundaries or limits. Boundaries are not walls, but they are protective devices that enable us to live with a strong sense of security. They include the "personal space" around you and how late people can call you. People with low self-esteem usually have no boundaries, and they let people take advantage of them. Limit-setting provides safe places and space for us to function. Every competitive sport has boundaries. When a play is out of bounds, play is stopped and only resumes within the boundaries of the stated game. We all draw lines in our life that we don't want others to cross. Emotionally healthy people have strong boundaries. They are not afraid to inform others where those lines fall. If you don't have any boundaries, you risk being run over emotionally, mentally, spiritually, psychologically, vocationally and humanly.

Do you need to do a little homework on your boundaries?

12. *Plan ahead as best you can, but know you will fail from time to time. When that happens, pick yourself up, find growth in the experience, and move on.* We all learn by trial and error. We all have the freedom to fail, but our plan should be to succeed.

13. *Be flexible, honest, patient, and impartial with a thick skin and a big heart.* This pretty well covers the landscape of blended family living and its demands.

14. *Keep communicating with honesty.* Yes, you can communicate in dishonest ways—and many do that. A good

rule is to be honest with God, honest with yourself, and honest with the other people in your world. And don't stop communicating!

15. *When things get tough, sit down and look through your wedding album together. It will remind you both of why you got married in the first place.* Going back to square one sometimes helps us move to square two. I suggest you keep your blended family wedding picture in a prominent place in your home where all family members can be reminded that you are family.

16. *Put God first in your life, then your marriage, then your children. Pray with each other, with your children, and by yourself.* God, marriage, children. Other agendas work hard to crowd that order out. For many people, it is job, children, school, church, and marriage. Review your order of priorities. Keeping them in order is instrumental to keeping your family growing and healthy.

17. *Use your love and faith in God and each other. Be patient and seek wisdom and forgiveness in your relationships as a family. Listen, pray, and look to the future as your blended family matures.* Reread chapter 4 on forgiveness. It's the glue to this advice.

18. *As a couple, stand strongly together so the children will know you are one. That way they will know they can't break down the relationship you have with each other.* All children everywhere at one time or another will try to divide one parent from the other so they can get something they want. It is called "divide and conquer," and children are skilled at playing that game. The game gets deadly when children try to turn one parent against the other parent.

Many children have worked long and hard to force a divorce in their blended family. I don't want to paint children as the enemy because the vast majority don't fall into that category. In all blended families, the father and the mother *must* form and *maintain* a united front. United you stand; divided you fall.

19. *Remember that you chose the new relationship; the children didn't. Give them plenty of time to adjust, adapt, and grow into the new blended family.* In a recent television reality show, three teens picked 1 woman out of 15 to marry their single dad. I don't think too many parents would go out and do likewise. Children are not adults with adult experiences and emotions. I can't quite envision them making what I consider a serious adult decision. Many children do not want their parents to remarry anyone, ever. Their secret hope is that their primary parents will get back together, and life will resume on the old familiar track. It is extremely hard for many children to face the reality that the reunion they dream of will never happen, and their father or mother will choose to marry someone else. About the only time children want a new parent in their lives is when the old parent was highly dysfunctional and caused them to live in a very unhappy home.

Give the children time. Love them through the adjustment process, which may go on for a very long time.

20. *Respect the children's feelings toward each other. Recognize there will be conflict between them at times.* If you are in a blended family where all the children involved love and care about each other and conflict is at a minimum, count your blessings. You are part of a small, select group. Some children will click and relate well to each other, some never

will no matter how hard you try to make it happen. Respecting feelings doesn't mean you will have the same feelings or that the feelings you do have are wrong. As one blended family dad said, "The goal in our family is simple: Peace!"

21. *Make every member of the family feel just as important and just as loved as every other member.* How do you do that? You start by saying "I love you" to all the children involved, all the time, and back up your words with acts of kindness. This means saying it to those who are difficult to love as well as to those who are easy to love.

22. *Discuss in detail each parent's role in child discipline, and make sure each child has a clear picture of each parent's role.* This is where a lot of unfairness can get into the blended family system. If there is no agreed upon disciplinary structure or if favoritism is shown to some children, you will find yourself in a war that will only get worse. Fair and equal discipline presented by a united team of parents will work. If you are not working at it, you had better start now.

23. *Respect the children's feelings toward their biological parent. Don't try to replace that parent.* You may not like him or her, but you need to keep those feelings to yourself. After a couple of years in your blended family, you may like them a lot less for all the stress they have caused you and your family. Stay out of that war. There is nothing there for you to win.

24. *Have one-on-one time with each of the children. Listen to them and emphasize their importance in the family unit.* If you are not doing that, start. If you are doing it, keep it going.

25. *If possible, nurture the relationship with the biological parent in order to reduce the stress in the children.* Sounds like going into the lion's den, but I watch this being done in many blended families, and it really does work. The plan is not to be one big, happy family. The plan is to not go to war every day with the children's biological parents. If you can do this, tension declines.

26. *Never criticize the biological parent in front of the children.* Actually, never criticize the biological parent period. Criticism can keep the wounds fresh and prevent healing. Remember, somebody loves the person you criticize.

27. *The children did not cause the breakup that landed them in a blended family. You and your former spouse did.* So keep them in the guilt-free zone. The children of a divorce usually have enough of their own guilt to last a lifetime. They have no vote in living out the choices other people make. They are often the refugees. They need to be treated with love and tender care. If they are, they will do great in life.

FOR DISCUSSION AND PERSONAL RESPONSE

1. In this chapter, what spoke the loudest to you?*

2. How do you plan to implement that in your life?

3. What difference do you feel that will make in your personal life or in the life of your blended family?

4. Who can you call on to help you and hold you accountable to bring that to reailty?

5. List three action steps you will take as a result of reading this chapter.

6. What key role will this chapter play in the long-term growth and development of your blended family?

THIRTEEN

The Most Asked Questions

W HEN WE ENTER UNCHARTED territory we have a lot of questions about what comes next. Most people want to do the right thing for everyone involved in their situation. One of the best sources of good, honest information comes from the people who have already been where we are going. Having a strong support group around us is essential to being an effective and successful blended family.

Through hundreds of sessions with blended family parents and members, I have tried to field the questions they have asked with practical answers. Here are some of the most asked questions followed by my responses, based on my experience.

Q. *Is there a big difference between marrying someone who has lost a mate by death and one who has lost a mate by divorce?*

A. Yes. Sometimes the one who has lost a mate by death wants to enshrine that person in heart and home and refuses to allow a new mate and new family into that space. Members trying to blend find themselves in a never-ending battle of putting memories to rest and combating constant comparisons with the deceased mate. This often raises its head in the dating experience, but is ignored by the about-to-be mate who thinks the old memories will be obliterated by building new memories. Old memories, if they are good ones, die slowly. With time most people eventually come to realistic terms with the shadows cast by the former mate. If not, it will be very difficult for the new blended family to survive.

Q. *Can a new marriage/blended family work if one partner has children and the other has never been married or had children?*

A. Yes, but it means a major adjustment will have to take place for all the people involved. The never-married-before person lives a "do what you want when you want to do it" lifestyle. Thinking for just yourself is vastly different than thinking for an entire family unit. Children in this kind of blended family are often looked upon as nuisances rather than family by the never-married new stepparent. The new spouse may want to spend consummate amounts of time with his or her new mate at the exclusion of the children. It is extremely difficult to become an instant parent with no previous practice. It can be accomplished though.

When I am involved in performing a wedding for that kind of blended family, I work hard with the one who was single. I want to know if he or she is ready to give up some things and take on new responsibilities. Many men and women with no prior marriage and child-raising responsibilities take on the role of playmate to the children, leaving the role of parent to the primary spouse. If this isn't talked about and looked at honestly before the marriage, it will be extremely difficult to work with after the marriage takes place. This is where premarital counseling is vital. If you have this problem and your blended family is already under sail, get some counseling help before the struggle gets out of control.

Q. *What about age differences between married partners?*

A. The May–December marriage is more common today than it ever has been. Older men marry younger women and start a third family. Older women marry younger men with the same result. The "yours, mine, and ours" seldom merits a raised eyebrow anymore.

The trophy wife–child bride syndrome may work fine when the bride is 24 and the groom is 44. The real problems come when the age difference is 44 and 64 or 64 and 84. Few people think long and hard about what lies down the road. What often lies down the road is another divorce when age starts to negatively affect the older mate.

Blending children into a family structure where one parent is only a few years removed from their own age can cause incredible disrespect and tension in the day-to-day life of the blended family. What goes into the blender doesn't always blend well with the other ingredients. That is not to say that any blended family with wide age differences in the adults will not work. I have witnessed those that have worked exceptionally well. But I have also witnessed those that quickly crumbled and added more debris to the lives of those trying to be a blended family.

The strongest question I can ask in an age-difference marriage is, "Is this an ego trip or is this a relationship built on solid love? Are you willing to work hard to make a new family work?"

Q. *What about changing the last name of the children in a blended family to that of your new husband?*

A. Since this usually applies only to the woman's children, it can be a topic that causes wide conflict unless resolved early. A legal process is involved in having a child's name changed. An identity problem is involved for the child when this happens. The primary father in most states must give consent to the name change. A primary rule of thumb is that once children reach school age, it is too late to tack new last names to them. Divorced fathers often feel they would be giving up their children when their children's names are changed; it would chop a branch off their family tree. Even when a father dies and the mother remarries, many children prefer to continue to carry their primary parent's last name.

I had a tough battle with my last name being that of a father I never knew while my sister had my stepfather's name. I was forever explaining why our names were different and wondered for many years why my new father did not "adopt" me and give me his last name. In this day of frequent divorces and remarriages, this isn't such a big issue.

The decision to change or not to change a last name for a child must respect the child's feelings. There is no right or wrong here. Sometimes it has to be talked out with the help of a wise counselor who can help those involved look at all sides.

Q. *How do you deal with a blended family that refuses to accept you as a new member of that unit?*

A. I talked about this in chapter 7 on acceptance. This can be a real problem in some blended family systems. The cruelest part of any rejection is that you are isolated and left out of important family events outside of your immediate blended family. You often get a "heads up" of what your future holds prior to your marriage. When you know that there will be some blatant rejection of you once you are a permanent part of the new blended family, you need to ask yourself if you can live with that long term. If you can't, reconsider your marriage plans. If you can and you know it may never change, proceed cautiously.

Q. *What do you do with "bouncing" children?*

A. Children have a way of testing a new structure. If they don't like it, you may hear them say "I want to go live with my father (mother)." Then, when living with the other parent becomes a problem, they want to move back with you. You can live with the "yo yo" effect only so long and maintain a balance in your blended family home. Continuity in living must be established for growth in the children to take place. All parents must agree that this must happen. Bouncing children can push you into land mines really fast. When final decisions are made as to where the children will live, those decisions must be enforced.

Q. *How do you deal with stepchildren who, when they come to live with you, won't abide by your rules and disciplines?*

A. Seldom are all discipline patterns alike. Everyone has their own hooks and twists. In order for a blended family to live in a healthy balance, house rules must be spelled out lovingly and followed diligently or you will find yourself in the battle zone. Everyone needs to be on the same page on this. You are responsible for the ground rules in your house. You are not responsible for the lack of ground rules in your stepchildren's other house. Life is good when everyone works together, but from my experience, that doesn't always happen. Complaining about what someone else does never solves the problem. You can only take responsibility for what happens in your own ball park. Talk with your spouse. Make sure you both agree on how discipline will be handled. Then present a united front to your children.

Q. *What happens in your blended family when a long-lost former spouse reappears in the lives of your children and wants life to be "wonderful" again?*

A. Few former spouses totally vanish from the face of the earth. Many former spouses have a habit of popping up at inopportune times and causing unrest, mostly with the children. You are divorced from that person, but your children are not. You can set ground rules in your backyard for the pop-up spouse that your children won't want to keep. Remember, it's your backyard and *you* set the rules, not your former spouse and your children. I believe children have the right to have the relationship they want with a former parent, but that does not mean the former parent has the right to cause chaos in your life. There is a fine line here, and both parents in a blended family need to keep a plan of action handy for close encounters of a disrupting time.

Q. *Are prenuptial agreements wise or do they tend to invalidate trust?*

A. In many instances they are wise. If you have inherited money or have money set aside for your children's education, I believe it is wise to separate this from what becomes common property in a marriage. When people are contemplating a second marriage, this is when this issue should be faced and decided upon. It is a little too late once the new family has been formed, but you can still seek legal counsel.

Q. *What role does a new spouse play when his or her spouse gets into a conflict with a former spouse?*

A. This issue comes up frequently in blended families. Conflicts do involve people who are outside of the conflict zone. It is easy to say "not my problem," but that doesn't make the problem disappear. Some former spouses even demand help from their former spouses when a problem comes up in their own lives. The former spouse who keeps running back to help gets in deep weeds with his or her new spouse and blended family member. Perhaps the best rule of thumb is the biblical mandate "be kind to one another." Being kind is often misunderstood as being taken advantage of. Those random acts of kindness are not exempt from the disturbing people in your life, whoever they may be.

Q. *How do you blend your Christian children with your new spouse's children who are not Christian?*

A. The most convincing part of one's belief system is in how it is lived out on a daily basis. You cannot superimpose your Christian beliefs on people who don't understand what you are talking about. I believe this is where the "love one another" command shows up best. You set the pace of your faith by how you live it out in your blended family. Those who are watching will either be intrigued by it or turned off completely. The tough part for most blended families who want to create a Christian home is having members from a former family question and mock what you are trying to build. Christian faith presented in a positive and loving way is contagious. You cannot change your stepchildren's home, but you can impact them with yours.

Q. *How do you keep from being resentful when a huge chunk of your spouse's paycheck goes to support his or her primary children and yours suffer because of it?*

A. You can build a quick list of resentments in every kind of family system. You can end up by screaming "It isn't fair!" 20 times a day. And in many instances, you would be right because many things in life simply are not fair. If you are a scorekeeper person, you will have more losses than wins on any given day. Somewhere in this maze of unfair things, you will need to begin counting your blessings. The blended family always comes with carrying charges. You will always be paying some bills that you did not cause or profit from. You should have been aware of any of those going into your marriage, and you should be prepared for the ones no one expected long after your blended family was formed.

Many members of blended families live with bad and unfair judgments placed upon their lives by a legal system that has only a small reputation for fairness. Sometimes those legal decisions involve a questionable distribution of money that can incur your wrath for years to come. One always has to ask the question when in disagreement, "Is this a hill to die on?" Do I use my time and energy to fight a battle I cannot win? Are there more important things that demand my attention?

These are only a few of the questions I have heard over the years. Some of the ones you may be asking right now need to go to the ears of a gifted and wise counselor or passed on to blended family friends in the form of prayer requests.

The questions do come less frequently after several years of a blended family existence. When I asked a blended family father recently how things were going, he said their family had been formed long enough to now experience what every other family experiences in the way of struggling times and celebrating times. He stated he wanted to live long enough to forget his family was ever a blended family. Good thought!

FOR DISCUSSION AND PERSONAL RESPONSE

1. In this chapter, what spoke the loudest to you?*

2. How do you plan to implement that in your life?

3. What difference do you feel that will make in your personal life or in the life of your blended family?

4. Who can you call on to help you and hold you accountable to bring that to reailty?

5. List three action steps you will take as a result of reading this chapter.

6. What key role will this chapter play in the long-term growth and development of your blended family?

FOURTEEN

Questions in the Minds
of Blended Family Children

I N THE FORMING AND MAINTAINING of blended families, children are often the least informed about the questions and concerns they have. Too often they are subjected to the plans and desires of the adults and are left with many personal fears and uncertainties that only increase with the passing of time. Children are no different than adults; they fear what they don't have specific answers to. Once they can get some answers, they feel less threatened and less insecure in a blended family environment.

The following questions are from my conversations with children prior to and living in a newly formed blended family. Your children may have a different list of questions, and they need to have the freedom to ask them, discuss them, and find some answers that will make them feel at ease.

Q. *What will my place be in this blended family?*

A. One of the strongest needs all children have is to know they belong somewhere and to someone. The disruption of a primary family system due to death or divorce leaves a child, regardless of age, in limbo. Any sense of family, home, safety, and belonging disappear quickly. School-work can suffer, and disobedience and acting out can become commonplace. About the only exception to these feelings and their outcome is from children who lived in chaotic and life-threatening situations. They are usually so happy and relieved that any new living situation would be welcomed without question.

If a child is the oldest of the children in a primary family, there is an accepted stability of that role and its importance. When the child goes from that place of status to perhaps becoming the youngest in a blended family, the adjustment and treatment of the new role can be difficult and unacceptable.

The roles of children invariably change in the forming of blended families. I believe the task of both parents is to help children find places where they fit well into the new family system. The battle of the sexes can add to the struggle to belong and fit in. Blending an all-boy family with an all-female family will demand a huge behavioral change for all involved. If there is no opportunity for both sides to express questions and feelings, you can find your-self living in a war zone.

Having the children involved in the creation of a blended family spend time with each other long before that family is formed is vital and important to its success. Not all children will welcome the possibility of blending their lives and future under the same roof. Getting feel-ings, objections, fears, and thoughts on the discussion table is vital to this new formation. Don't be like the two adults who went to Las Vegas, got married, came home, and informed the children on both sides they would now all be moving into the father's home. That's not blending; that's colliding! All children want to know how they will fit into a new structure. Talk about it openly. Ask questions and listen to the responses. Let your children ask questions and express their thoughts and concerns.

Q. *What will I gain, what will I lose?*

A. Most of us live for the "wins" in life and tolerate the "losses." Children are no different. They want to know what becoming a part of a new family will bring into their lives in the win column. Better housing and their own room usually top the list of wins, followed by better school, new friends, and improved economics. Some children in new blended families feel they have moved up a notch in lifestyle while others feel they have moved downward. Losing friendships and peer support groups is a loss no child welcomes. Moving out of town, state, or country can be the most traumatic event in any child's life. Loss of acceptance and the fear of never being accepted is often stronger outside of the blended family unit than inside.

I have listened to too many blended family parents trying to convince their children that this new adventure will be wonderful for them when in reality it is only wonderful for the adults. Again, children need to be able to question, talk, and share feelings in order to understand and accept change. They need to express themselves about what they feel they will gain and what they will lose. I have met parents who will not take a job promotion or transfer unless their children agree with it. You may not agree with that, but I believe it has merit because their world will change as much as yours.

The loss for everyone in creating a new family is losing forever the primary family structure. For the adults involved, the fact they have found a new spouse makes their loss disappear more quickly. Children stay connected to their primary parent in most cases, but the relationship often changes. Some primary parents draw even closer to their children, while others remarry and form new families and drift away from their birth children.

Winning is its own celebration. Losing sticks around for a long time and finds no quick replacement to alleviate the pain. Blended families can never guarantee that everyone involved will always win and never lose.

Q. *How will my new stepparent impact my life?*

A. A child may never ask this question out loud, but it lies in the back of his or her mind. In a primary family, the parent and child are there from birth onward. How that parent impacts the child is second nature. A blended family stepparent is an unknown quantity because there is no history to fall back on. Too many stepparents totally forget this fact and simply live like they were always present in the stepchild's life. The longer you are physically present in the life of that child, the greater your impact.

In blended family weddings, I ask both parents to make personal commitments to each other's children. Sometimes they give each child a remembrance gift after they make their verbal commitment. The impact for any stepparent starts right there. From then on, it's a day-to-day challenge. I believe the new parent first needs to tell stepchildren how he or she wants to impact their lives. By doing that, the parent is answering the never-asked question for the child and also making a lifelong commitment.

Q. *What do I do now about my birth parent and me?*

A. I believe that question is best answered by another question. What kind of relationship does the child want to have with his primary mother or father who is no longer in the day-to-day mix of his family? Once that has been decided, that parent has to be informed of the child's desires and respond. Relationships travel crooked pathways for all of us. They become more intricate in blended family systems. I believe that stating the desire for any relationship is first and primary to the success of that relationship. It is often the desire of the blended family parent of his or her children to want them to honor, love, and obey their new stepparent and leave the primary parent in the dust somewhere. That choice belongs to the children. They should be free to make their own decisions.

When the court systems in many states agree upon joint or shared custody after a divorce, they are trying to give children equal access to both parents. I believe in both birth parents being involved in their children's lives except when a parent might endanger or be harmful to the children.

Q. *What if I don't fit this new blended family team?*

A. Fitting in involves both the child and the stepparent. I believe they are equally responsible to make that work. Teens are often most resistant to the process and tend to disregard the feelings and desires of stepparents who want to bridge the gap. Many teens hold rigidly to their primary parent connection and may even express their desire to live with them. Younger children seem to move more easily into blended family structures. Parents in a blended family need to decide early on to help their children fit the new system. It takes time, energy, honesty, and lots of love. I believe a genuine desire to love, accept, and care for someone else's children will make them feel they fit this new family. It will take time.

Q. *Will I be able to follow the new rules?*

A. The parent who tells a child to follow certain rules "because I say so" needs to join the marines. Bringing new rules into a new system is trouble enough. But playing the role of general to your troops will win you no rewards. Rules no longer in effect and new ones that take their place need to be talked through with the children. Reasons and purposes need to be explained so that everyone is on the same page. When blended family parents disagree on house rules and disciplinary structures, the family will fracture, arguments will ensue, and the children will end up living to evade the adult arguments. Changing rules from day to day never wins the day but brings confusion to everyone.

Rules are guidelines for living and should be set in motion to help everyone do better. If you never talked about disciplinary structures before you entered your blended family, you better stop and talk about them now—and include your children in the conversations. They need to help form the rules they agree to play by. Remember, people support what they help create, children included!

Q. *What if this doesn't work?*

A. When a marriage fails and a family divides, there is always an inherent fear that a second marriage/blended family may go the way of the first. The failure rate of second marriages is higher than that of first marriages. There is often a nervous edge around the adults in a second marriage. I have listened to that fearful feeling from children as well. The destroyers that lurk around first marriages are multiplied in second marriages. The risk is greater, the issues larger, and there are usually more players involved. I am not trying to scare you, I just want to keep you plugged in to reality.

When children survive a family break-up, they often wonder if they can trust a second family to work out. They also become skeptical about their own chances of someday building a happy family. Doubt is always out there when you have been hurt once. There are no insurance policies against the failure of any marriage. Second marriages appear to have more land mines hidden in the underbrush than do first marriages.

Becoming a team in a blended family is the first step to getting everyone invested in making the blended family strong and failure proof. I watch strong blended families working hard to grow stronger when the standard of success is owned by everyone. I believe a team of parents can say, "Many blended families fail, but if we are all working at making this a success, we will not fail." That's a strong message to send to children wondering about the future.

Q. *What if the love changes in our blended family?*

A. I have watched hundreds of single-again men and women become great loving, caring, and productive single parents. I have watched them focus on their children and do great parenting jobs. When a remarriage is on the horizon and a blended family not far behind, children wonder if the attention given by their parents will now go to the new stepparent, and they will be left on the sidelines. Truthfully, that sometimes happens, but usually only when the parents become self-focused rather than family-focused. When you live in a spouse-free zone for a long time, having a new spouse makes you thankful and desirous of giving that person much of your love and attention. I have had children tell me their mom or dad were madly in love...but not with them. When attention is diverted, children get hurt. There is no question that parents should love each other. They just need to make sure that their children are not left out in their new venture into euphoria and togetherness.

One of the great losses in a new blended family is to be left out of the circle of love. Children feel that almost instantly. It is seldom intentional but needs to be carefully watched for. Saying "I love you" often and with meaning helps keep love at the center of your family.

Q. *What happens if you are an older married child with your own family when your single-again parent remarries and creates a blended family?*

A. I will long remember the young couple who sat in my office and informed me their mother had chosen to remarry into a blended family structure. Their question to me was, "How can we prevent this from happening?" My short answer, "You can't," seemed to offer them no solution. They were totally opposed to the way this would impact the primary family, even though their parents had been divorced for a long time. They had built their own case against the about-to-be stepparent. They wanted no additions to their family tree, and they were out to sever the branch before it got connected.

Older children who now have their own children can become very controlling about what happens to their parents. Their basic desire is to return to the good old days in their memories. Remember the chapter on acceptance? If you are stuck here, reread it. I know it is not easy to accept what you consider intruders into your family system, but that choice belongs to your parent.

I have seen two kinds of faces at wedding ceremonies over the years. Happy ones and angry ones. That picture has seldom changed over the years of working in this field. Happy is glad for this new twist in the life of someone you love. Angry is wishing something else was happening rather than this wedding.

Children of all ages have many questions when it comes to joining a blended family. You may not have answers for all of them as the involved parents but you do owe a listening ear to the questions and even an attempted answer to the best of your ability. Creating and living in a blended family is a whole new world of untraveled territory for most members of the family. Listen to the questions your children ask, and hear the ones they are not asking.

The following powerful feelings were expressed by a teenage friend of mine who experienced a divorce in her family and shared her thoughts about a future stepfather.

Hello. Is it you?
How do I know you won't be like the last—
and leave like the last?
Will you really be there—
when it's cold or when I'm scared?
Will you be the one to catch me when I fall,
to let me cry and feel my pain?
Will you laugh and hold my hand as if to say,
"I'm here and I will always be."
Can you take the time to get to know me
and learn to love me?
Will you leave the busy day behind and share my life with me,
and let me share yours with you?
Will your arms always be open to my yearning embrace?

Will you let me cry when the whole world is my enemy?
And will you hold me just as tight
* when the world is within my grasp?*
Will you be proud of the person I have become?
It's sad, you know, for you weren't there to see me grow.
You weren't there to bandage my wounds or the broken hearts
* and dreams of my childhood.*
For all you know is the person I am now.
The last one was there, you know.
He saw me fall as he turned and walked away.
So the father that helped create me
* was never really my Dad.*
Is that who you will be?

—Jennifer Dillon

FOR DISCUSSION AND PERSONAL RESPONSE

1. In this chapter, what spoke the loudest to you?*

2. How do you plan to implement that in your life?

3. What difference do you feel that will make in your personal life or in the life of your blended family?

4. Who can you call on to help you and hold you accountable to bring that to reailty?

5. List three action steps you will take as a result of reading this chapter.

6. What key role will this chapter play in the long-term growth and development of your blended family?

FIFTEEN

How to Create a Blended Family Support Group

THROUGHOUT THIS BOOK I have emphasized how important having a support group is to your living and growing in a blended family. Because I have worked in the field of single adult ministries for so many years, I know that one of the strongest needs in a person's life after the loss of a spouse through death or divorce is a support system. For myriad reasons, within a year of your loss of a spouse, you can lose up to 80 percent of the support you had when you lived in the world of married people. That loss can leave you pretty much alone in facing tough transitions and changes. The finding and rebuilding of a support system takes time and a full-on search. Because I have been a pastor for 45 years, I think one of the best places to turn to for that rebuilding is your church. I also realize in making that recommendation that many churches are very insensitive to the needs of widowed, divorced, and never-married single adults. If a church is not willing to meet needs and bring healing in those areas, there is even less of a chance that they will be attuned to the needs of blended families.

When I travel and speak in other churches, I spend a lot of time trying to convince pastors of the needs in these areas. Some respond by pledging to start singles ministries, while others use the oft-spoken excuse, "We are under-staffed and cannot commit any pastoral energy to that area."

If you are currently attending a church that does not have a blended family ministry, here are a few suggestions that may help you get one started.

1. Get two or three couples living in blended families together for a talk time with the senior pastor. Share the blended family struggles and journeys with him, and ask for his help in starting this ministry. Emphasize why you feel you need it and what you are personally willing to do to get it started. I believe the ownership of a blended family ministry should rest in the hands of its members. You need the vocal support from the senior pastor, but you do not need him to add one more job to his schedule. If he can assign a staff pastor to give you support, make sure that staff pastor meets with you to listen to your stories, vision, and concern for blended families.

2. Announce in your church bulletin that you plan to start a blended family ministry, schedule an invitational meeting for prospective members, and share your dream with them. Emphasize that a blended family includes the entire family unit, not just the adults. You don't need a long and involved battle plan at that meeting. You are simply casting a vision and asking others if they will share that vision with you. Get names, addresses, phone numbers, and email addresses before the meeting ends. Ask those present what they feel they would like to contribute in the

way of gifts, talents, and skills to help build this ministry. End your meeting with a time of prayer, asking God to give clear directions. Set a time for your next meeting to lay out a plan of action for building a ministry team that can carry the ball and make things happen. Remember, you need a *team* to do the job right. Leadership must be shared to be effective, although you will need a point person or two on every team to generate enthusiasm and action.

3. One of the best questions to ask those desirous of being involved is, "What kind of ministry would attract you and cause you to want to be involved?" And then, ask "What would that ministry look like?" Dream a ministry that envisions great things happening to its participants. Talk about ways to invite new people and make them feel welcomed. Ask what the needs of blended families are in your group, and plan things that speak to those needs. Never assume you know—always ask. When a ministry is meeting needs, people will be attracted to it.

4. Are you saying, "Okay, I want to be a part of this kind of ministry. Tell me what to do and I will do it"? I could list 25 things you could do based on the groups I have worked with, but that would be assuming that your group is like mine. The needs may be similar, but the ways of meeting those needs are uniquely yours. Your ministry needs its own identity and fit. Giving it a name is also important. Having a purpose statement tied to the name will tell people what your group is all about.

5. Since children play a vital part of blended family life, it is important for them to meet other children from blended families. Having social events, sports events, camping trips, and so forth are good tools to allow that to happen. Yes,

there is a time when parents need to talk to other parents in the blended family world without the children present. My rule is to plan 50 percent of what you do with children and 50 percent without children. I have met groups that never include the children and just talk about their problems all the time. Don't fall into that trap because it makes your group problem-oriented and does nothing to make the children feel vital and important.

6. Network with other blended family groups in your area. Find out what they are doing, and plan to do some things with them. If there are no other groups around, help start some new ones in other churches or communities.

7. If your church is not interested in helping you form a blended family ministry, I recommend you do it outside of the church on your own. Or find a church that is sympathetic to your dreams and vision. I know that sounds a little rebellious, but I have little patience with churches and pastors who are unwilling to help fulfill needs that their people have.

8. Beware of the pastor who tells you to simply join some existing married couples ministry in your church. The differences and struggles between primary families and blended families are at opposite poles. Many people I have met around the country have told me that is what their pastors suggested, and they were unwilling to understand the difference. Blended family people know the differences and need kindred spirits in their journey.

9. There are many resources today that can help you form a blended family ministry. I've listed some of them under Resources at the back of this book. Websites, books,

and specialist counselors are available to you. My personal feeling is that any church and every church needs a blended family ministry. Please understand that there is a vast difference between a ministry and a program. Programs assume the needs, while ministries create answers to the needs that stand out after asking people, "How can we help you create a stronger and healthier blended family?"

10. There is a gravitational pull among people living in a blended family. A "me, too" spirit makes them unique and different from primary families. We all face some of the same things in family living, but the blended family has its own specialized challenges. Families meeting together is the first step to meeting those challenges, so it's important to congregate.

11. Become a resource person for your blended family ministry team by collecting helpful materials that you can pass along to help other families grow. Because of the growing number of blended families in our culture, each month numerous magazines present helpful ways to improve living. New books are being published every year that can be used as discussion material for your study group. New websites with helpful information are also available. All you need to do is go to the search engine Google.com and type in stepfamilies, hit Search, and you will have more information than you can ever use. Become a collector of helpful things to encourage others in the development and health of blended families.

12. Create a "Blended Family Prayer Collage" to remind you to pray for each other. One blended family group had a picture day at their church. Each family was photographed with enough prints per family so that all

blended families could have their own copies of everyone's family as a visual prayer reminder. One individual family made a wire circular frame and attached all their blended family friends' pictures to it with the words PRAY FOR in the middle.

There are many ways to create a dynamic and caring blended family ministry in your church or community. If it is not being done, don't wait for someone else to do it. Step up and answer the call. It will be worth the work!

For Discussion and Personal Response

1. In this chapter, what spoke the loudest to you?*

2. How do you plan to implement that in your life?

3. What difference do you feel that will make in your personal life or in the life of your blended family?

4. Who can you call on to help you and hold you accountable to bring that to reailty?

5. List three action steps you will take as a result of reading this chapter.

6. What key role will this chapter play in the long-term growth and development of your blended family?

SIXTEEN

Goals for Your
Blended Family

IF YOU AND I COULD have a one-on-one conversation today, we would not talk very long before I would ask you to share some goals you have for your blended family. You might respond with a blank look and wonder why any goals you might have would be of any interest to me. I want to help people explore, dream, envision, and establish goals for their own lives and the lives of the family members they are involved with. I have watched too many exciting new beginnings take place when a new blended family is formed, only to be followed by the onset of routine living and surviving with no goals and objectives to work toward. Goals, large or small, give meaning and purpose to our lives. The fulfillment of goals gives reason for celebration and life. Without any celebration, life will become routine and boring.

Some wise person said that there are three basic things that constitute happiness in our lives: something to do, someone to love, and something to look forward to. We can live a day here and there with one or two of those missing, but we cannot live a life without those three things filtering through our days and nights. The "something to look forward to" part involves the things ahead of us that we plan for, look forward to, and enjoy doing when the time arrives.

It is becoming more difficult in our society to switch gears from the "must do" list to the "want to do" list. Making a living takes precedence over our desire to "make a life." Keeping schedules other people set for us squeezes the things we want to do right off our daily pages. Laying out a few plans and goals for our future not only seems impractical but virtually impossible. I want to challenge you in this chapter to stop long enough to think about the kinds of goals you can work on, and then look at some areas you can form goals around.

I believe a blended family husband and wife need three sets of goals. First would come the personal goals one has for oneself. Second would be the goals the parents have for themselves as a couple. Third, the goals that are formed by the entire family unit for the family. If you fail to target these areas with goals, you will end up 20 years later on the "wishing" side of your life. Here's a grid for good understanding and processing.

1. Always write down any goals you make in a notebook, daily planner, or journal. Writing them down is like pouring concrete around them. They are no longer dodging in and out of your brain. They are visually in your lifescope and clearly identified. I live with a daily planner that includes all my goals. Wherever I go, my planner and my goals go with me. When I see them in print, I work on them. Planners help you stay organized and effective on a daily basis. When you reach a goal, plan a celebration and cross that goal off your list. Replace that goal with a new challenge.

2. Make the goals you set for yourself highly personal. You can share them with anyone you choose to for some accountability, but you have to be the proprietor. It is harder to set personal goals than goals for anything else. Getting in shape physically, losing weight, setting spiritual disciplines, getting further education all involve *you* taking up the challenge. You are your goals. You may need some people to fall in step with you if they have similar goals. Losing weight often works more effectively when you do it with others. There is a certain degree of strength in community. Very few of us make good Lone Rangers when we are pursuing goals. We need the affirmation of others along with our own measuring stick. One of the first things I work on with clients in life coaching is helping them clarify and prioritize their goals. My personal goal is to help my clients. Their personal goal should be to help themselves move from where they are to where they want to be.

When you lose sight of personal goals and have no magnets drawing you toward your future, you can quickly fall into survival mode, which is closely followed by the death of your spirit. Can you name two personal goals you have right now in your life? If not, you have some homework to do.

3. Most forms of goal-setting fall into three break points: long term, mid term, and short term. The length of time in each of these areas can be decided upon when you set the goal. Too many people pick long-term, way-down-the-road goals, so they don't have to do anything about them right now. Have you ever noticed that people who plan to start a diet always say they will start tomorrow as they peer down at the array of food on the brunch tables? A long-term goal for you might be something that will

take two or three years to accomplish. A mid-term goal could be something within a current year, while a short-term goal would fall into the weeks or months category. You have to set reasonable parameters that will work and be attainable. Too many people set unattainable goals so they will not have to work at them or, when they do, they will demolish themselves in the process.

Goals have steps you can attain with hard work and effort. You don't throw a goal up in the air and hope it will stick somewhere. Anybody can set those kind. Set goals that you can honestly work on and attain. For instance, I would love to run a marathon. I have been a runner for years and usually run a few miles every day. In order for me to run a marathon, I need to first face the question, "Is it physically possible at my age and state of health?" If my doctor says yes, then I face the all-too-miserable training regimen that will enable me to enter the marathon. If I enter it, my goal is to finish it. If I can finish it, I want to do it in hours rather than days.

Remember, if all your goals are long term, there will be no "high fives" for a long time, and you need those "high fives" along the way to keep you going. Break long-term goals into short, attainable goals, and spread them out so you won't be left out of the celebrations along the way.

4. Be wary of setting up contingency goals. Contingency goals have too many outside variables you cannot control. A contingency goal says, "I will do this if…these ten other things fall in line." You cannot control the other ten things, and you can be quickly torpedoed and cast up on the beach while others are building their sand castles.

Some people plan contingency goals so they can blame others for goal failures. If you are not careful, you can blame all your goals away. Highly successful people are often no smarter than you are, but setting and attaining their goals makes the difference between success and failure. Avoid any goal that is anchored in contingencies. You are not called to wish upon a star. Anchor your wishes in goals that are reachable, and you will be rewarded.

5. Share the goals you set with others, not to brag but to gain assistance in accomplishing them. When you share a goal with other people, you come out of hiding and invite them to ask you how you are doing as you move toward reaching it. It's fun and a challenge to share goals within your blended family. It invites family members to get involved. They can keep you accountable. If you haven't come to this conclusion by now, let me rip off your blinders and say *it's all about the team.* Teamwork helps you get to your goals. To accomplish all the keys to being a healthy blended family, you need a team. To achieve your goals and their goals, you need a team.

6. Affirmation is the adrenaline that keeps us in hot pursuit of our goals. Affirmation says, "You done good!"

Remember when your children went to kindergarten and brought home the first pictures they drew? They wanted them glued forever on the refrigerator door. What they wanted more was for you to tell them the pictures were wonderful, and you were so proud they drew them for you. They wanted your approval, and they will still want it when they are 50. Our need for human affirmation never goes away. People authenticate our existence when they give us any form of recognition. For instance, when someone says, "Thank you for your book. It really helped me," it affirms me and propels me to keep writing. If someone says,

"Dumb book," I wonder if everyone feels the same and consider ending my writing career. We all collect enough "downers" in life. We need the affirmers close by to let us know that our goals and objectives are on target. Working toward your goals should invite affirmation from others, which should also set you free to affirm their goals.

7. Set goals that make you stretch. If your goals neatly fit your comfort zone, they will not stretch you. Safe and attainable goals do not raise the challenge bar. "Stretch goals" demand you reach inside yourself and take your life to another level. Magazines and newspapers are filled with stories of successful people who pushed the envelope goal-wise and reached new heights. Children in any family system will look to the adults for models of goal-reaching. A good example will motivate them and keep them stretching. A poor model will send the message that goals are trivial and not important.

Injured athletes who have gone through rehabilitation and returned to the playing field often cite their parents as models of setting and attaining goals. Members of a blended family often carry their own injuries from the failure of their primary family. They look to the new family as both a healing place, a safe place, a stretching place, and a place where their goals can be realized.

Some of the great blended family stories I have listened to over the years involve stepparents who raised the goal bar in families and caused their stepchildren to accept the challenge to raise their own bars.

If you took a quiet 30 minutes right now, what areas of your life would you list that need formative goals? There are always the urgent and demanding things that pop up first. They form more of a "to do" list than a goal list. For starters, let me suggest nine areas of your life and the life of your blended family where goal-setting could move your family forward.

Relational Goals

Relational goals begin with asking the question, "Who do we have in our lives relationally who nourish us and make us more productive as a family?" Coupled with that is a second question, "Who do we have in our lives relationally who are toxic to our existence and deplete our energies?"

I mentioned earlier that divorce or death of a spouse causes you to lose many of your married friends. When you form new friendships with other single-again people, you rebuild your community, only to lose that community when you remarry and create a blended family. Being in a blended family community is very different than being in a primary family community. As you rebuild, it can be a time to look at your circles of relationships. Who do you need to invite in, and who needs to be invited out?

A relationship review for your entire family unit is vital and important to your growth. People need to be in a community where they have a sense of belonging, understanding, and being cared for. They need to be receivers as well as givers in that community. If you are in a community of takers, you will eventually be depleted and burned out.

One of the healthier things we can do is review and set relational goals and then work intentionally on those goals. Charlie Brown in the comic strip Peanuts often says, "I need all the friends I can get!" That is true for all of us! God has created us to live in context and community with one another. That takes reaching out as well as reaching in.

The next time you have a family discussion, ask each person to name his or her friends and what he or she gives to each and what the friend gives back. You can follow that by asking what kind of friends they feel in need of that they don't have. You will have great dinner table discussions when feelings about friendships are honestly shared.

Three basic relationship types exist in our lives: casual, close, and intimate. The casual area involves the "floating" people in our lives that we know, but don't know very well and don't want to know very well. The close friends are usually the people built into our social structure. They are the people we do things with. We may know them well or only a little, but we need them because doing everything alone is no fun. Intimate friends are comprised of our inner circle of people who know everything about us, we know everything about them, and some strange mystical thread continually strengthens that relationship. The span of years and miles never ends that kind of relationship. We only have room in our inner circle for a handful of people because those relationships demand time, energy, and care. Enduring relationships are valuable and need nurturing and preservation. New friends can be welcomed in our lives, but few will fall into the intimate category.

What kind of relational goals do you need to set for yourself, for you and your spouse, and for your family? Be intentional as you set those goals!

Personal Goals

Personal goals turn the focus on *you*. We talked about this earlier in the kinds of goals we need to set. I would like you to think about what you need to do to continue your personal growth and what you can personally do to help the growth of your family. For instance, if you feel your blended family needs to focus more on academic education, are you willing to take the lead in that area and set the example? School is never out for any of us, as long as we are alive. Class is always in session because we need to learn and grow.

If there is a weight problem in your family, are you willing to set the pace in setting some personal goals of weight loss? Too often, parents tell children what to do, but they seldom say, "Follow me. I'll do it too."

If there is no spiritual center in your family, are you willing to set the pace and example to establish that as your personal goal? Jesus took personal responsibility for his growth. Luke 2:52 says, "And Jesus grew in wisdom and stature, and in favor with God and men." I believe this verse refers to four areas of life: mental, social, physical, and spiritual. When you work on all four, you will find that your life is balanced. Where are you on the spiritual balance beam? What personal goals do you need to set that, when attained, will help both you and your family?

Vocational Goals

Vocational goals can come out of the answer to this question: "Does your job cause you more happiness than unhappiness?" If your job, career, vocation has you mired in unhappiness, it will impact every other area of your life. Many men and women do not go to work each day with a feeling of joy, challenge, optimism, and expectancy. If you are one of those, may I ask you a question? What could you do career-wise that would be a fulfilling of your deepest passion? Is getting there and doing that an impossible dream? Are you willing to look at your life and do an honest review of the vocational part? Are you willing to set some goals and take some steps toward a vocation change? Marsha Sinetar has written a book titled *Do What You Want and the Money Will Follow*. Her premise is simple: You will be happy doing what you love to do, and you will be able to make a living doing it. Changing course midstream vocationally in today's world is more commonplace than ever before. Age is irrelevant; your passion is relevant. But this is not a knee-jerk decision or spur-of-the-moment goal. You need someone by your shoulder asking you the tough questions and helping you explore your options. Making a vocation change is a process that takes time, thought, energy, and prayer.

A great part of any family's happiness comes from the people within it. Blended families are no exception. An unfulfilling vocation can lead to complaining and criticizing. A steady home diet of that will cast a cloud of daily gloom over a family's growth and productivity. If you are happy in your career, you can set positive goals for advancement.

Financial Goals

Financial goals are closely related to vocational goals. If you are financially successful in your career, it is easier to set financial goals that will positively impact your family and its future. Blended families often carry an excessive financial burden if money goes out to aid primary family members. That can go on for years until the children graduate from college. As one friend recently said, "My problem is not setting financial goals. It's dealing with financial overload that loves to hang around with me."

Plotting and planning your financial road usually require some wise outside assistance. I have referred many people in my ministry travels to Crown Financial Ministries to assist them with financial planning. (Crown Financial Ministries can be reached at 770-534-1000 or at www.crown.org.) Some blended families get so loaded with credit card debt that they need outside help to extract them from that burden. Too many families crash on the rocks of financial ruin and end up with another divorce.

Money always tops the list of blended family concerns in small group discussions. Setting realistic and practical goals in this area is vital to survival. You need to be extracted from a financial mess before you can set solid goals for your family in this area. I have two words for you if there is a problem in this area: *Get help!*

Educational Goals

Educational goals are important in the lives of your blended family children and your primary family children. The solution to the rising cost of education is impacting every family today. Many blended families I have worked with don't even want to talk about it. Avoiding education issues does not resolve it however. I believe there are always solutions when creative minds are at work. For instance, community colleges are cheaper than private colleges. The computer is fast becoming the teacher in many areas of education. Working at forming educational goals for your family members will be hard work. You may have to include yourself for further education if you are changing careers. Adult education in community colleges today is a growing field. Many classes now have more people over 30 than under 30!

Have you looked at your family's education needs? Is it time to set some goals?

Family Goals

Family goals demand family participation. All family members should be sharing their own goals and allowing them to become part of the blended family's bigger goals. Children understand what goals are. Academics and sports put goals in front of them early on. Teaching them to personalize a few goals is easier than you think. Just don't give them too long a list to work on. One at a time works best.

After establishing the personal goals of each family member comes the need to have some goals for the entire family. Those goals need to encompass all the members. One goal might be for a family to plan and save for three years for a trip to Europe. Every member gets to do a part, and they all contribute to the family as a unit. A friend of mine shared a goal his family fulfilled when he was a teenager. The family decided they wanted to take a year off and sail around the world. They planned for several years, read books, studied maps, learned sailing, and watched videos of where they were going. And they went! He said he would never forget the experience and what it did for his family. He took the same goal-setting principles into his own family.

Creativity needs to flow through family goals, whatever they are. If you are living in a blended family right now, what are some family goals you have set out to pursue? What dreams do you have that can become a reality? What memories do you want your family to share that will last a lifetime? When do you plan to talk with your blended family about goals?

Health Goals

Health goals can be highly personal and interpersonal within your family. Let me start with you. What kind of shape are you in physically? What kind of shape do you want to be in physically? Do you eat right, exercise, and take care of your greatest gift—your body? Are you an example of a healthy person to your blended family members? Are you ready to set some goals and lead by example for your family in this area? What are your family's needs in the health area? This is a huge issue to think about and work on. It demands a high degree of discipline after you set your goals. You will treat your health in one of two ways: by design or by default.

Maybe your family needs a healthy activity you can do together, along with what they do individually. Mountain biking is gaining importance as a family event. Nutrition is gaining in importance as a guide to better health. In today's world of wellness and disease prevention, there are more tools available to help you to better health than ever before. But America is still the most obese nation on earth. That does not say much for setting healthy goals. Is it time to take health goals seriously? Yes! What is your first one?

Emotional Goals

Emotional goals involve a very important question: How emotionally healthy is your blended family? That may be a difficult question for you to answer. All the members on the road to becoming a blended family have usually gone through an emotional wringer prior to arriving at their destination. One of my biggest concerns in performing a blended family marriage ceremony is what kind of emotional shape the about-to-be-blended members are in. They always look good, smell good, act good, and smile a lot, but I wonder what's rippling beneath the surface. I pray that everyone is in good shape emotionally and that the new family has a great chance to survive, thrive, and grow together.

I know that the river of emotion runs deep and wide in every blended family system. Unresolved issues bubble to the surface, and new issues that strain emotions fight to be heard. So what do you do when you discover emotional needs in your family? You try to enact some goals that will help find resolution for them. The question is simple: "How are you doing?" The answer might be "not so well." Then the question is, "Are you willing to get whatever help you need to do better?" Sometimes that help comes from a support group, sometimes from within a family, and at other times, from a therapist or counselor.

If there are emotional needs in your blended family that need taken care of, be willing to set some goals and work toward resolution.

Spiritual Goals

How are you and your blended family doing spiritually? I wrote about this earlier, but I do want to suggest here that you talk openly about spiritual goals for yourself and your family. If you have decided to follow God and you have a faith foundation to stand upon, setting some spiritual goals will help you build a superstructure on that foundation. Remember what Joshua said? "As for me and my household, we will serve the LORD." Can you say the same thing?

After thinking about these nine goals, you may be ready to add a few of your own. Goals become reality when you develop a plan to reach them and devote quality time to attaining them. Goal-setting is easier than working to reach them. You will need lots of help along the way. Don't be afraid to ask for it. Reaching goals helps you grow. An anonymous person summed up growth with these words:

> Growth is betrayal of arrangements that were,
>
>> Growth is change that is threatening as well as promising,
>
>>> Growth is denial of something and affirmation of something else,
>
>>>> Growth is dangerous and glorious insecurity.

If you want to grow, become a goal-oriented person in your blended family.

FOR DISCUSSION AND PERSONAL RESPONSE

1. In this chapter, what spoke the loudest to you?*

2. How do you plan to implement that in your life?

3. What difference do you feel that will make in your personal life or in the life of your blended family?

4. Who can you call on to help you and hold you accountable to bring that to reailty?

5. List three action steps you will take as a result of reading this chapter.

6. What key role will this chapter play in the long-term growth and development of your blended family?

SEVENTEEN

Blended Families and Estate Planning

by J.J. Thomason, CFP
Long Beach, CA

W HILE ESTATE PLANNING CAN BE complex for all families, it can be especially complex for blended families. In addition to considering your spouse and children from your current marriage, both you and your spouse may have children from prior marriages. Consider these tips:*

Sit down with your spouse and discuss both of your desires. Make a list of assets you each brought into the marriage, as well as assets obtained after your marriage. Discuss how you want these assets distributed after your deaths. How will you address children from prior marriages? Will you each make your own provisions or will you consider all of the children jointly? Once you and your spouse reach agreement, your estate-planning documents should support

---

* The information contained in this chapter is for general information only and does not constitute specific legal, accounting, or investment advice. Consult a financial planner for advice for your situation.

these decisions. Keep in mind that even if you have a will, your spouse can often override the terms and elect to receive a statutory percentage of your estate. To prevent this, you typically need a prenuptial or nuptial agreement.

Determine whether trusts are necessary to protect your children's inheritance. When assets are left outright to your spouse, he or she controls the ultimate distribution of those assets. You may want to use a qualified terminable interest property trust (commonly referred to as a QTIP trust) to protect your children's interests. Assets you designate are placed in the trust, with income distributed to your spouse during his or her lifetime. Since this usually qualifies for the unlimited marital deduction, no estate taxes will be paid when you die. After your spouse's death, the principal is distributed to your heirs.

Review beneficiary designations and life insurance amounts. It's not unusual to forget to update beneficiary designations for retirement accounts, individual retirement accounts, and life insurance policies. These assets will be distributed to your named beneficiaries, regardless of the terms of your estate-planning documents. Thus, take a look at those designations to ensure they are coordinated with your estate plans. Also review how much life insurance you have. You may need more to help ensure that *all* your heirs are treated equitably.

Check how your property is titled. Jointly owned property automatically passes to the co-owner. You cannot change this distribution through a will.

Discuss your plans with your family. You should communicate your estate plan, especially in situations with stepparents and stepchildren. You don't want your children to believe your spouse has unduly influenced you or you don't care about them. Being open and upfront about your estate plans will hopefully prevent disagreements and misunderstandings after your death.

For more information on financial planning or specifics on establishing trusts and other financial instruments, consult with your attorney or a professional investment advisor.

FOR DISCUSSION AND PERSONAL RESPONSE

1. In this chapter, what spoke the loudest to you?*

2. How do you plan to implement that in your life?

3. What difference do you feel that will make in your personal life or in the life of your blended family?

4. Who can you call on to help you and hold you accountable to bring that to reailty?

5. List three action steps you will take as a result of reading this chapter.

6. What key role will this chapter play in the long-term growth and development of your blended family?

Epilogue

REAL PEOPLE LIVE IN blended families. The following four personal accounts are just a little glimpse of people I know personally who have lived through the loss of a spouse by divorce or death, and eventually remarried and sucessfully blended two family units into one. These stories are shared in their own words with only light editing.

Family #1

My name is Stephanie, and I would like to share with you a brief story about my family, including all the ups, downs, and in-betweens. I was married to my first husband when I was 19. At the time I knew I was young, but I also knew I was in love and that love could conquer anything! Against the strong wishes of my parents, especially my mom, I got married. What I didn't realize was that I was marrying a man with a strong addiction to drugs and alcohol that I could not conquer for him nor he for himself. After seven years of marriage, we had our first son, Austin. He was the love of our lives. Four years later we had our second son, Logan. He also was the love of our lives, but by that time the alcohol use seemed to be escalating, and the rift in our marriage was growing deeper. After two years of this escalated roller coaster I realized it was time for me and my children to get out before too much harm was done to the boys and myself. My husband and I separated. I moved out and got my own place with the boys. After a while, my ex-husband really seemed to be trying hard to get his act together. He told me he was attending AA meetings and going to church, which he knew were the things I wanted to hear. So, after a year, I decided I would try to reconcile my marriage, which I had tried for so long to save. Not long after being back together as a family, I realized that nothing had changed except my husband's drug of choice. At the same time, I found out that I was pregnant, which was really shocking because it was not easy conceiving the first two times. At that point I knew I couldn't bring another child into this mess, so after a few months of really scary and awful times with my ex, I was able to get out with my boys. I moved into a bedroom that I rented from some friends. Five months later I delivered my third son, Dakota. He was the love of his brothers and my lives. The feeling of freedom we all felt to be away from my ex was huge. We were all very happy for what God had brought us through.

Some other people and I started a single parents group at the church we were attending. It was such a great place for not only the adults to meet and share so many similar problems we all faced, but for our children also. I always felt that God had drawn this group together to help lift and encourage each other, and in the process we all became such good friends. We had additional singles groups in our church, and in one of those groups I met my current husband, James. He is the love of all our lives, and my parents really approved this time.

James had never been married, and he had always wanted a big family. He even told his friends he wished he could meet someone with kids. I didn't date until I met James. I knew in my heart if there was a man for me out there God would put him in my path! It was a perfect match for the boys and James. They only saw their dad occasionally, and then not at all. They really needed a man in their lives. We were married on April 17, 1999. Several months before we were married, James went into business in the automotive industry with his longtime friend. The hours he had to put in were long, and sometimes I felt like a single parent again. But other than that, things couldn't have been better. The boys and James loved each other so much. I was so happy that when I met James he had never been married and had no children of his own. In dealing with my own ex and seeing my friends having to deal with exes on both sides, I felt very fortunate. Before James and I married, we had discussed his wanting a child. I agreed if it was something he really wanted. On August 8, 2000, we had a baby girl, Kendra Rose. I was ecstatic, I couldn't believe I finally had a girl. The boys loved her to pieces, and so did we. I used to say she was the glue that bonded us together as a family.

I know from experience that sometimes God has other plans for our lives, things that we cannot foresee for our future. One week after we dedicated our baby girl to the Lord, he took her unexpectedly from us. She died of SIDS on October 30. What a shock. What a blow to our family. Everyone, including us, asked how this could happen after all we had been through. I wondered how we would do without this baby to hold us together. This baby my husband had wanted for so long, and this girl I had always hoped for was gone so fast. But in reality, her death drew us all closer than we could have imagined. Through the strength God gave us, and the love of our friends, we were able to pull through okay! James and I had peace knowing that God had a bigger plan for us than we could see, and that he took our daughter for a reason. We laid up our treasures in heaven. Kendra is gone from us only temporarily, and we will see her again when we meet in heaven. Soon after that, James sold out his half of his partnership so that he could take a job that would allow him to spend more time with his family. God totally provided a job for James to enable him to be way more involved in the boys' lives and mine.

Nine months after the death of our daughter, the boys' biological father died suddenly. My first reaction was relief because I had always worried about what he might try to pull. However, I didn't know how the boys would react. They were actually as relieved as I was because they had been afraid of him. So the glue that I thought we had lost in our daughter had actually been given back to us in the death of the boys' father. It allowed us to move forward as a complete family. James could give the little corner of his heart he had not given to the boys because of the unknown factor of their dad coming back into their lives.

God closed one short chapter in our lives, but opened a huge new one. And I have to say that it seems weird even to me that we are not the original family from the get go. It just feels like we have always been together. James and I feel that we are really on this journey and maybe we can tell others how God has carried us through such low times in our marriage and lives and brought us to such higher places. Our marriage today is strong, but we still have our little struggles now and then for territory or power, but we are always able to come to a compromise, and then we move on. God definitely sent James into our lives and, as he likes to put it, "We were meant to be together." I just took a detour along the way!

Family #2

It's been nearly four-and-a-half years since we got married, and though many issues have been resolved, it seems that some never will. I think the greatest challenge we are faced with is one that all blended families face—trying to take an abnormal situation and make it as normal as possible. Whenever couples who are considering remarriage ask me for advice, I like to tell them, "Just remember, it's not the Brady Bunch." In most cases, as in ours, there is an ex-wife and an ex-husband in the picture. Because of that, there are usually three different households involved. This means three sets of rules, three styles of child-rearing, three (or, if you count additional stepparents, six) opinions and ideas about what is best for the children. My husband and I can establish a structured, loving, consistent, Christ-centered home, and be undermined at every turn by the other parents. This does not happen in every case, but it is still a frequent occurrence. We have learned that we can only control our own home, and pray for the children when they are not in it.

My husband and I have very different personalities. To make matters more challenging, I was raised in a Christian home with strict parents and my husband was not. We have very different styles of child-rearing. I have learned to lower my expectations slightly, and he has learned to raise the bar. I have also learned to give my opinion, but not demand that he follow it (bear in mind, this took years for me to figure out.) We have both learned to choose our battles carefully.

Another issue that we continue to have is the "his kids vs. my kid" syndrome. I believe we both try to be as fair as possible, but if either of us feels our child is being criticized or attacked in any way, we revert back to being protective single parents. It is also difficult on these occasions to discuss matters privately rather than in front of the children. Although we know that we should, emotions tend to take over, and we don't follow the rules we have set up for ourselves. Although these incidents have become less frequent, it is still a constant struggle.

My advice to anyone considering blending their families is to be patient and pray. Jesus could have been speaking directly to us when he told us to "pray without ceasing." My husband and I make an effort to be consistent with this, but it is difficult. I do know that when we make the time, we see a difference in the way we relate to each other and to the kids. Remember that regardless of your past, you and your husband are now united in God's eyes, and you are a family. Eliminate divorce as an option. When you and your spouse have disagreements, and you will, step back, take some time apart, and pray about resolution. As difficult as it may be, thank God for the difficult times because you have the opportunity to grow from them. You will be surprised how He will take seemingly impossible situations and teach you both about trusting Him.

Family #3

Scott was previously married for almost 10 years. His marriage ended when his wife went to be with the Lord in 1995 at the age of 41 years. Scott has two daughters from that marriage: Rachael, 29 years old (stepdaughter from his first marriage) and Jordan, 10 years old (adopted in first marriage).

I, Jolynn, was married in my late teens for two years. I have one son, Bill, who is 18 years old.

Scott and I met in February 2000, through a singles ministry at the church we both were attending. We dated for two years before getting married in August 2002.

We were fortunate that we didn't have to face some of the challenges that some of our friends face in second marriages. Most of all, we don't have to deal with ex-spouses, child support, and child custody issues being that one of our marriages ended in death and the other relationship was with a noninvolved birth father. Billy does have an adopted father that has been part of his life since age three, but both Billy's adopted father and I have no conflicts.

The main positive in our lives is that both Scott and I are grounded in the Lord and are committed to our marriage. We have a lot of love for the Lord, each other, and our children. One of the benefits was that we attended the same singles group at church that had speakers that spoke on relationships and blended family issues.

Another positive is that we have brought a balance to each other and our family. Scott was not consistent with his younger daughter regarding rules and discipline. I have brought consistency there. I have also brought a lot of other positive attributes that a woman brings to the home. Scott has recently been more involved in parenting my son, Bill, and is taking some of the burden off me. Previously I had been the one administering the guidance and discipline.

One of the major problems we have had is blending two households full of personal belongings. I got rid of all my furniture and some personal belongings. At the time that I moved into Scott's house, Scott had not dealt with his deceased wife's personal items, which has made me feel that he hasn't made room for me. This is something that Scott and I are still dealing with.

Another area that we need to work on is communication with each other.

Family #4

We have been married for 57 days! Let me tell you, it has been an adventure already. Between the two of us we have five children, ages 5, 7, 8, 10, and 16. We have them 100 percent of the time. In that aspect we are not like a lot of blended families because we don't get any weekend breaks. We don't have any ex-spouses in the picture. There are a lot of issues with both sets of kids. The feeling is mutual with all the kids though, "They are all happy to finally have a complete family." The kids have adjusted great. I think the one thing that has surprised us the most is the fact that the boys want to call me mom and the girls want to call Chuck, dad. That was something we did not expect, and something that certainly was never even going to be an issue. I think that in itself shows how happy the kids are.

It has been quite an adjustment for me. Everything has tripled...my laundry, cooking meals, packing lunches, etc. I was so overwhelmed the first week with keeping the house clean that we now have a house cleaner. I think my biggest challenge is going to be having to let certain things go. I have to realize that I can't do it all. I think the best advice I could give right now—the one thing I have learned so far but it's the one thing that is going to carry me through this journey (besides praying a whole lot!)—is *laughter*. I am going to have to have a really good sense of humor. I am learning to laugh at myself as well as at certain situations that come up. Chuck has had to adjust, too, but in a different way. Chuck has three boys, and I have two little girls. The look on his face the first time one of the girls cried to get something was hysterical. He really had no clue how to handle that. He still walks around the house saying, "Girls are sure different from boys." It has also been quite humorous for me to see a grown 40-year-old man sitting and having a tea party with painted fingernails and barrettes in his hair and his legs folded under the little table the girls have. There is no sight like it. Then there is Charlie, Chuck's oldest son, the "teenager." There is nothing like living with a teenager. I am amazed at all the things there are to be dramatic about. He is a good kid, but he drives me nuts with the drama and not remembering anything. So, Chuck is getting used to the drama with little girls, and I am getting used to the drama with a teenager.

We have had the typical issues that come along with a big blended family...close the door when going to the bathroom, knock before entering a room, don't walk around in your underwear, etc. So far we haven't had anything too embarrassing happen. Ask me again in a year, and I am sure I will have a story or two for you.

I truly feel that we have been blessed. Chuck and I have learned so much from facilitating Divorce Recovery and Kids Hope workshops. We really tried to apply all the things we learned with our family. I know we will have issues as we go along, but I feel like we have all the right tools, support, and knowledge to handle anything that is thrown our way.

The most important thing, though, is our faith. We pray as a family. We live our lives being faithful to God and trusting Him. There is nothing more important, and that is what will give our family strength and love and patience and all of the other things we will need to grow and succeed in all we do.

FOR DISCUSSION AND PERSONAL RESPONSE

1. In this chapter, what spoke the loudest to you?*

2. How do you plan to implement that in your life?

3. What difference do you feel that will make in your personal life or in the life of your blended family?

4. Who can you call on to help you and hold you accountable to bring that to reailty?

5. List three action steps you will take as a result of reading this chapter.

6. What key role will this chapter play in the long-term growth and development of your blended family?

Resources

WITH THE ADVENT OF the computer and the ability to search thoroughly for any information on any topic under the sun, I want to give you a few basic recommendations and set you free to explore additional helpful resources. Check out two key websites:

1. instepministries.com—Located in Tucson, Arizona, counselor and author Jeff Parziale has created several excellent books and study guides for blended families.

2. saafamilies.org—The Stepfamily Association of America is the grandparent organization and resource center for a lot of helpful information. They are also publishers of the bimonthly magazine *Your Stepfamily*.

For helpful links to the many stepfamily sites, go to any of the search engines, such as Google, and type in "stepfamilies." You will quickly discover what is available.

Additional Helpful Reading

Becoming Family: How to Build a Stepfamily That Really Works, by Robert H. Lauer, Jeanette C. Lauer

Family Rules: Helping Stepfamilies & Single Parents Build Happy Homes, by Jeannette Lofas

How to Win as a Stepfamily, by Emily B. Visher, John S. Visher

Living in a Step-Family Without Getting Stepped On: Helping Your Children Survive, by Kevin Leman

Stepfamilies: Let's Talk About It, by Fred Rogers

Stepfamilies: Love, Marriage & Parenting in the First Decade, by James H. Bray, John Kelly

Stepfamily Life Can Be Hell but It Doesn't Have to Be: 7 Steps to Recreating Family, by Annette T. Brandes

The Truth About Stepfamilies: Real American Stepfamilies Speak Out About What Works, by Anne O'Connor

What Am I Doing in a Step-Family? by Claire G. Berman

Journal

Date_____

Journal

Date_____

JOURNAL

Date_____

Journal

Date_____

Journal

Date_____

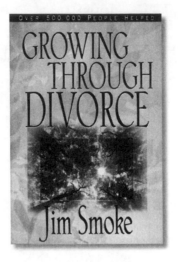

More than 500,000 people have been helped by Jim Smoke's *Growing Through Divorce!*

Divorce is one of the most painful and emotionally draining experinces that a human being can have. It is a hurt that goes deep and is accompanied by the doubt that it will ever heal. *Growing Through Divorce* offers compassion and practical guidance for anyone facing divorce. Based on Jim Smoke's firsthand experience of working with thousands of formerly married persons, this book can transform your life from an old ending to a new beginning! Includes a helpful "working guide."

If you have any questions or would like to discuss the key principles in *Seven Keys to a Healthy Blended Family* or *Growing Through Divorce*, Jim Smoke can be contacted via e-mail at:

JSmoke1745@aol.com